£2.50

Leading Ladies

Leading Ladies

CONVERSATIONS WITH :

DAME PEGGY ASHCROFT
DAME EDITH EVANS
HERMIONE GINGOLD
JOAN GREENWOOD
DAME CELIA JOHNSON
ELSA LANCHESTER
BEATRICE LILLIE
RACHEL ROBERTS
DAME FLORA ROBSON
DAME MARGARET RUTHERFORD
DAME SYBIL THORNDIKE
ESTELLE WINWOOD

BOZE HADLEIGH

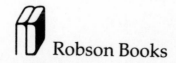
Robson Books

First published in Great Britain in 1992 by
Robson Books Ltd, Bolsover House, 5–6
Clipstone Street, London W1P 7EB

**British Library Cataloguing-in-Publication
Data**
A catalogue record for this book is
available from the British Library

ISBN 0 86051 808 6

Photoset in Berling by Derek Doyle &
Associates, Mold, Clwyd. Printed in Great
Britain by St Edmundsbury Press Ltd, Bury
St Edmunds, Suffolk

In Loving Memory of
A Great Woman and Lady,
FLORA BELLE STOCKWELL BOZE

Contents

Acknowledgements

Heartfelt thanks to Ronald M. Boze, Fresia Garcia Lyon and Linda Fresia.

Special thanks to Jordan R. Young for helping bring these twelve 'great dames' home to Britain, and to photo collector, fan and friend Doug McClelland.

Thanks also to: Cecil Beaton, Alf Conner, David Corkill, Jackie Corkill, Gilbert Gibson, Rose Hellman, John Inman, Christopher Isherwood, Elena Kellner, Jim Kepner, Samuel Korda, John Lehmann, Robert Patrick, Jim Pinkston, Mary Renault, Tony Richardson, George Rose and Julia and Mary Stockwell.

Introduction

We shall not see their like again: a dozen 'leading ladies' of stage and screen, most international stars, half of them Dames of the British Empire, about half born during the reign of Queen Victoria. From Ashcroft to Winwood, nearly all lived to a ripe old age – their eighties or nineties or past a hundred – performing well and frequently, regardless of age or billing.

These 'great dames', as I fondly remember them, conquered the stage and screen, usually via talent rather than beauty. Their brilliant careers were thus epochal instead of flash-in-the-pan. Artistry was their aim, not sudden stardom or immense wealth. Dedication was their route to success, and so their acclaim was sincere, not fashionable.

Today, when careers are often measured by a handful of films or a single, typically mediocre, mega-hit, we can appreciate the longevity of these women's accomplishments. Their unique portrayals endure in the national consciousness, in individual memory, revival cinemas, television and videocassette. The actresses' lengthy careers spanned their salad days to a mature harvest of plum roles to a golden rain of honours, awards and legend.

Some of them were superb tragediennes, others beloved comediennes. Some created immortal screen characterizations, others lived their lives and legends primarily on the stage. Most did not commence their careers with the temporary advantage of classic looks, therefore their careers only increased in praiseworthiness. Most of these thespians attained their professional peak and their widest popularity long after forty.

These profiles unveil an impressive gallery of varied leading ladies whom we've all seen and admired since childhood. Their humour, wit and candour illuminate the times and personalities of the gilded age of British acting and entertainment. In each encounter, it was my intention to reveal the woman behind the leading lady so that her essence and specialness could be preserved in time and on the printed page.

Had I not been part-English, I would still have been an Anglophile and devotee of British drama and literature. My mother and maternal grandfather lived in post-War London for a few years, and I heard wonderful stories about the local theatre and actors. Eventually I was able to meet various now-historic figures of British culture, some of whom became interview subjects. I particularly sought out the 'great dames'. Although I grew up less than one hundred miles from Hollywood, I was more intrigued by UK actresses than domestic favourites who often declined after the age of thirty.

In Los Angeles, I delved into the cult of personality by acquainting the likes of Elsa Lanchester, Rachel Roberts and Estelle Winwood. In New York, Hermione Gingold. And in Britain, the majority of these ageless, wondrous and fascinating women. Some were intimidating, but sometimes I was bold, even daring, in my questions, and perhaps my gender and youth allowed me to probe where older and possibly jaded journalists wouldn't or couldn't.

In some cases, it took years to effect an interview. I was lucky in my connections on both continents, and in impressing upon the actresses concerned my sincerity about their work. I was honest in noting that in most cases our session might not yield a published interview in American magazines or newspapers, for whom beauty is the desired commodity for an actress and local television or mainstream films the desired vehicle.

When later I decided on a book-length collection of interviews, I realized that for a considerable chunk of the American public, even that which reads books, it could be deemed too 'foreign'. Or of the past.

But in all cases, the result of my meetings with these famous and revered British actresses was exciting, nostalgic, intimate and surprising.

I have tried here to allow each woman to speak for herself via her answers and also her evasions. I've included what I feel to be the necessary amount of facts and observations about each performer's career, interspersed with her self-evaluation and comments about her professional and private lives.

Today, when every other person who goes before the cameras is termed a 'star', when even 'superstars' work but once every two or three years, and when quantity not quality determines who is a so-called legend, it is pleasing and comforting to recall the heyday of valuable entertainment when – as one of these leading ladies put it – the best special effect was talent.

1

Dame Peggy Ashcroft

Self-admittedly not 'adept' at interviews, Dame Peggy Ashcroft acceded to my interview requests which commenced in 1982 after seeing her as the Countess of Rousillon in All's Well That Ends Well *at London's Barbican Theatre. I made one request a year until she agreed in 1986, after winning an Academy Award for* A Passage to India *(1984), becoming famous on three continents in the 1984 teleseries* The Jewel in the Crown, *and recently playing Agatha Christie for TV in* Murder By the Book. *The interview, once embarked on – at the home of a Canadian friend – proved second nature to the excellent actress.*

The first topic covered was Agatha Christie, and the extent to which Dame Peggy identified with the author whose repetitiveness was both a challenge and a bottomless goldmine. 'We all must ask ourselves if we're not boring our audience? The challenge is to cut a new pattern from the same old cloth. I have only myself to work with. Mrs Christie had her chosen genre, with all its rules and limitations. Added to them were her own limitations of class, era and so forth.

'It goes without saying that the greater challenge is to devise an entire story, with all its components, characters

1

and plot twists, and its logical summation, than to take a single character and bring her to life. For an actress, the words already exist. They should give her motivations, movement, carriage ... If the character is well-written, the actress's work is less a chore than a happy task. It might also be a pleasant, or in any event a surprising, self-discovery, although this is more and more rare. Oh, dear. I hope I don't sound like an instructress?'

Who better to be instructed by, I said.

'To conclude this comparision, it is a lighter task for an actress than for someone like Mrs Christie. I do not feel inclined to jealousy of a talented writer, which she was, particularly one who had to restrict her creative expression to one genre. There were so many expectations of her! From her publishers, her readers, the mystery arbiters, the young fans daring her not to bore them ... It's a marvel that her well of creativity never ran dry. She would most likely have continued writing a novel per year had she lived even longer than she did.

'But she did have one sizeable advantage over an actress: she could generate new characters each time out. Or change the setting altogether, though she seems seldom to have done this. An actress or actor, by comparison, has only his physical self to work with. His mental exertions may be fewer than the author's, but it is his or her body out on the stage. It is her face and presence which must not bore the theatre audience through over-familiarity. In motion pictures, a stellar personality may be expected to repeat itself, but most stage actors fear creating monotony. We need the help of a good playwright, but from within ourselves we must summon up a newness or differentness each time out of the gate, so to speak.' She twinkled shyly.

In *Murder By the Book*, as Christie, Dame Peggy co-starred with Ian Holm as the writer's most famous creation, Hercule Poirot. The amusing and elegantly acted plot concerns her desire to kill him off, thereby sparing herself and her readers an increasingly decrepit monotony. But in so doing, argues the indignant, even terrified Poirot, she would murder part of her creativity and her professional heritage.

'I imagine your portrayal of her would really have pleased Mrs Christie,' I noted.

'Do you think so?'

'I can't think of another actress she'd rather have in the role.'

The actress raised a qualifying finger. 'Being portrayed at all couldn't have been much to her taste.'

'Did you know her well?'

'I don't expect any actor knew the late Mrs Christie very well. She was exceedingly private, and came from a time when respectable people didn't *know* actors.'

'Do you think she was biased against actors?'

'I would venture that she was intrigued by the profession … dazzled by the personalities who enacted her characters on the stage and screen. At the same time, she very likely chose not to become too close to any given actor, in light of her shyness and the old social barriers.'

'When we think of actresses who are also ladies, we in America often think of British actresses. Yet, as you point out, a *lady* like Mrs Christie would to some degree have looked down her nose at most actresses …'

'It seems unfair, doesn't it?' Dame Peggy smiled maternally. 'Nowadays, actors may earn a great deal of money – although it is not by any means a steady profession for most. Nor was it then, before you were born. There was, besides, the stigma of an actress frequently having to kiss a man other than her husband – for the stage. That was viewed dimly indeed.'

'Women had very few career options?'

'Few options, and stereotyped ones. There were the good professions – to be a nurse or teacher. Or the bad ones – actress or good-time girl. Not much else.'

'Surely, it's changed tremendously?'

'It has, although the golden era for actresses seems to be behind us now. You might even look upon me as something of a dinosaur!' She laughed gently. 'But indeed it has changed. Even if it hadn't, I would still be an actress, and still take great pleasure and pride in it.'

'May I ask what you consider your greatest asset as a performer?'

'Oh, my. Let me think … my persistence, I think. It is true of many of us.'

'And your greatest shortcoming, if any?'

'You're too kind … the first shortcoming which enters my mind is that, by nature, I am too easily a part of the background.'

'You blend in too easily?'

A quick, firm nod.

'Some would call it naturalism.'

She politely demurred. 'Others would say, quite correctly too, that I haven't a star personality.' I demurred. 'It's true, though. It is true,' she smiled beatifically.

For a Dame who confidently claimed to have no star personality, Peggy Ashcroft could also claim a long list of achievements. Though not truly famous until old age, she was counted as a distinguished and consummate stage professional. As a woman not blessed – or accursed – with star looks or personality, she played the gamut as a working actress: queen, prostitute, rat-catcher, nun, alcoholic, teacher, ghost, landlady, even a Chinese businessman! She created roles in plays by Somerset Maugham, Terence Rattigan, Clemence Dane, John Drinkwater, John Home and so on. 'I'd love to have created roles for my favourite of favourites,' she intoned, adding that she would however have to have been male to have played Shakespeare's immortal women.

'When people hear the word "actress", they assume magical things. Things such as glamour and a life of ease and adulation. Far more so even than actors, actresses have had an arduous and even perilous journey through the centuries when actresses have been permitted to exist at all.' Asked why she believed actresses were once so scandalous an idea, she replied: 'Women had less than a handful of life roles: it was a revolutionary concept that a woman could choose a variety of roles and emotions, and be applauded and paid for excelling at them. Apart from which, learning lines implied literacy, even a good education, and the Church could subordinate ignorant women more easily than educated ones. The times have not changed that much.'

Dame Peggy was born Edith Margaret Emily Ashcroft on 22 December 1907 at Croydon in Surrey. Her father, an estate agent, was killed in the Great War. Her mother was a devoted non-professional actress who sadly did not live to see Peggy become a professional one. At sixteen, she attended the Central School of Speech Training and Dramatic Art, whose founder and principal was Elsie Fogerty. Her final examination found her doing a scene from *The Merchant of Venice*. Actress Athene Seyler singled out Peggy and co-performer Laurence Olivier for their budding talent.

Peggy had long since been appearing in Shakespearian plays, often in male roles. At eighteen, she made her professional bow in Birmingham in James Barrie's *Dear Brutus*, as a dream-child. Ralph Richardson was her stage father. A year later, she played another daughter in John Drinkwater's first comedy, *Bird in Hand*. She co-starred with Olivier.

In 1927, she made her West End début as a maid in Congreve's *The Way of the World*, also understudying Edith Evans's acclaimed Millamant. Her biggest break to date occurred in 1929, in *Jew Süss*. Ms Ashcroft essayed Naemi. Critic Harold Hobson remarked on her 'voice of unimaginable beauty'. Later, the actress modestly asserted that one could not go too far wrong in a part in which she read from the Book of Solomon and protected her maidenhead by leaping to her death backwards off a balcony.

On the strength of her Naemi, the fast-rising stage star

was cast by Paul Robeson as Desdemona in his controversial *Othello*. Also in 1930, she played in Somerset Maugham's *The Breadwinner*, then did several West End drawing-room comedies which failed to satisfy her or her audiences. But the following year, at a mere twenty-four, she was chosen the leading lady of the Old Vic, taking on meaty and widely seen roles by Shakespeare, Shaw, Goldsmith and Sheridan. Yet in the middle of that busy season – ten parts in nine months – she made time to star at the Little Theatre in Schnitzler's *Fräulein Elsa*, a characterization twice as long as *Hamlet*. 'Energy,' she softly stated, 'is its own reward.'

In 1933, ironically the year of Hitler's election to power, Ashcroft made her screen début in *The Wandering Jew*. (It was re-edited and re-released in 1939 as *A People Eternal*.) German screen star Conrad Veidt played the lead, with Ashcroft as the prostitute who unknowingly betrays him to the Inquisition.

In 1986 Dame Peggy explained: 'It was – is – in many ways a naïve film. In spite of the ghastly events taking place during that era, the cinema was not at all egalitarian. It experienced difficulty in reconciling itself to the simple fact that a minority of people is no worse or better than, but only different from, the majority.

'For all that, I was flattered whenever I was approached to be in a picture. It was a novelty and rather a thrill, for quite a long time … *still*,' she beamed.

(In Hollywood, Veidt recalled 'Miss Ashcroft's intensity, a lovely impact which grows in remembrance and should not be wasted on the immediacy of celluloid.')

Dame Peggy's film career encompassed little over a dozen efforts, and her characters were invariably supporting ones. But she was directed by Alfred Hitchcock, Berthold Viertel, Anthony Asquith, Carol Reed, Fred Zinnemann, Joseph Losey, Peter Hall, John Schlesinger, Maximilian Schell, Tony Richardson, James Ivory and David Lean – a list enviable to many actresses with five times the number of movie credits.

In 1934, Ashcroft took on a one-act play written by Pirandello for Eleanora Duse which Duse never performed, *The Life That I Gave Him*. In 1935 she did her second film, no longer looking like an *ingénue*, as Mrs Crofter in *The Thirty-Nine Steps*, helmed by Hitchcock. It was a minor role, but 'Hitch' predicted a shining career for her because 'the greatest thing about her is her extreme simplicity'.

Also in 1935, the stage leading lady acted alternately opposite John Gielgud and Laurence Olivier in the former's legendary production of *Romeo and Juliet*. Its 189 performances at the New Theatre broke all records for a Shakespeare play. W.A. Darlington of the *Daily Telegraph* deemed Ashcroft's 'the finest and sweetest Juliet of our time'. Her youth – unusual in that youthful role! – was a bonus. Next year witnessed another triumph, Nina in *The Seagull*, the West End's first full-scale staging of a Chekhov play. The production was directed by no less than Theodore Komisarjevsky (who was Ashcroft's second husband, between 1934 and 1937).

I inquired what it was like working with Gielgud?

'Bliss!' She clapped her hands. 'Sir John is ... superlative. Sensitive on the stage and off the stage. Had he never opened his mouth to act, he would have been renowned ... an extremely generous director and performer.' How did he compare with Olivier as an actor? 'As actors, both produce utter sincerity. Of course each has a different personality through which his performances are filtered ... both have magnificent voices.'

How did Gielgud and Olivier compare as directors?

'I do not compare directors.' She lowered her lids and shook her head. 'It would be fruitless. I will say: John has received nowhere near enough credit for his contributions to the theatre. His contributions to the New and Queen's Theatre seasons were crucial to what evolved after the war. He has possibly a less glittering command than Larry. He is at least as talented, but possibly has less flash to attract the eye of, shall we say, the more publicity-minded.'

As for Komisarjevsky, 'He was awesome at first. As with Sir John, you would need to work with him and read at least some of the books about him – memoirs too – in order to grasp how monumental a stage figure and presence he was. I attribute much, and possibly most, of my success to working with people of that stature.' She was quiet for a time, then wondered aloud, 'There were more giants then – I'm not sure why …'

In 1936 Ashcroft appeared in Berthold Viertel's film *Rhodes of Africa* (just *Rhodes* in USA). She offered, 'There is a delightful novel, a short one, by Christopher Isherwood, *Prater Violet*, based upon his experiences writing for Mr Viertel. Do read it – it was another world, and Mr Viertel was a charming although worldly director.'

In the 1940s, the actress participated in only three motion pictures: *Channel Incident* (1940) and *Quiet Wedding* (1941; both helmed by Anthony Asquith, the latter co-written by Terence Rattigan), and the 1942 *New Lot*, directed by Carol Reed, and her last film for sixteen years.

'There is more variety on the screen, in the sense that on the stage we cannot go on location. There is more which can be presented upon the screen, sometimes more realistically. The range of directors, their personalities and methods, is also more varied, and there is always the star temperament to consider. There is a recognized pecking order. The stage is more fraternal. It is rooted more in hard work and talent.

'Younger journalists want to know why I've done so relatively few pictures. I say that I've done more than I'd intended, and more than I would have thought I'd be asked to do! At the time, they seemed just a pleasant diversion, something to alternate with the theatre, in a secondary, even light-hearted way – I did my best, as all stage professionals do, but I never considered that what I was doing for the screen was of primary importance to myself or anyone else.

'The fact that it continues to exist is the ongoing reward of film. Its perpetuity offers repeated pleasure to the fans of a given picture, and I must say it is riveting, even awesome, to stare at oneself as one was so long ago!'

Which was her favourite of her films?

'That would be immodest … I will let you know a few [other people's] pictures which I have thoroughly enjoyed. Of course you may not be familiar with their principals. Long ago, there was *Jassy*, which starred Margaret Lockwood and Patricia Roc. Very glamorous, exciting, you know. Also at that time, in the 1940s, one entitled *Madonna of the Seven Moons*. It had Phyllis Calvert in it, also Patricia Roc. Wonderfully made and effective pictures. In the *Madonna* one, Phyllis enacted two wildly differing personalities – one a gypsy and the other, a sedate housewife. I did envy her such an opportunity!'

Why, I asked, did some British actresses, like Deborah Kerr and Greer Garson, become Hollywood stars, while others, such as Lockwood or Calvert, didn't?

Dame Peggy threw up her hands in perplexity. 'I can only imagine that it was a question of luck. The ladies you have named were all lovely and talented … Being in a very popular picture time after time must have made the difference.'

Did she ever envy those stars?

'No,' she smiled. 'Their runs were generally rather short. One can experience a longer run on the stage – a less worrisome one too, I imagine. That, apart from the matter of so-called stars losing all practical right to their privacy and – again, so I would imagine – their peace of mind. I may now and again envy an actress a particular role or her triumph in a particular role. I have, though, been fortunate in never envying another actress her career. Mine has suited me very well.'

In 1937, Ashcroft journeyed to New York to star on Broadway in Maxwell Anderson's *High Tor*, directed by Guthrie McClintic. More satisfying was the 1937-8 season at the Queen's in London, overseen by John Gielgud. This included *The Merchant of Venice*, in which Peggy's youth again provided notable contrast with the older actresses who typically essayed Portia. She moved from Shakespeare to Sheridan to Chekhov to Oscar Wilde with ease. In 1939 and 1942, she scored a popular success as Cecily in Gielgud's productions of *The Importance of Being Earnest*.

Less successful was Stephen Haggard's *Weep For the Spring*, an anti-Nazi play that did not make it to London in 1939, or Clemence Dane's 1940 Edith Evans vehicle *Cousin Muriel*, with Ashcroft and Alec Guinness poorly reviewed as young sweethearts. By war's end, she was back in Gielgud's capable hands, at the Haymarket, in *Hamlet*, *A Midsummer Night's Dream* and *The Duchess of Malfi* (she repeated this role fifteen years later).

Because of her youthful figure and countenance, Peggy Ashcroft inhabited younger roles for many years. She broke that pattern in 1947-8 by starring in the hit drama *Edward, My Son* as a middle-aged alcoholic. In 1949 she tackled Catherine Sloper, the forlorn spinster in the classic *The Heiress*, helmed by Gielgud at the Haymarket. Sir John then guided her through *Much Ado About Nothing* and *King Lear* in the 1950 season of the Shakespeare Memorial Theatre Company at Stratford-upon-Avon.

In 1950 the war-damaged Old Vic reopened, and Ashcroft's Viola in *Twelfth Night* was the expected sensation. The *News Chronicle*'s Alan Dent rhapsodized, 'With her flower-like grace and bird-like eloquence, I have all week been in a state of breathless adoration.' In 1951 the Old Vic afforded Ashcroft a chance to play Greek tragedy, as *Electra*, for one of her favourite directors, Michel Saint-Denis. With middle age, her range was expanding, to great praise. She later explained: 'Age can force us out of a routine which may have become comfortable but may be boring theatre-goers and stifling one's creative growth ... Taking a chance on something different can be a fearful process, but whether it is labelled a success or a failure, it is its own reward.'

Another break with her *ingénue* past was a 1952 play penned by gay playwright Terence Rattigan. Originally, *The

Deep Blue Sea was about an older and a younger man, but at the time, homosexual themes were banned from public stages and performed solely in 'private' or club theatres. Rattigan thus rewrote − as Tennessee Williams sometimes did − the older man as a female character. He offered it to Peggy, who declined it because she felt no sympathy for the older woman's yen for a young man.

Rattigan divulged the legal reason for the character alteration and, with 'Binkie' Beaumont's aid, persuaded the actress to accept the project. 'One cannot put one's friends or relatives in the forefront of one's mind when considering a role that may shock. One must think of the more sophisticated among the audience, and of the creative call to combat!'

The following year found the varied star back at Stratford, with Michael Redgrave. First as Portia − for the last time − then somewhat improbably as the queen of the Nile in *Antony and Cleopatra*. The critics were divided about her credibility as the Egyptian vamp, with Kenneth Tynan dubbing her a 'Cleopatra from Sloane Square'. However, the consensus was that she had done better than expected.

'I did not undertake Cleopatra in order to elicit good notices or any pats on the back,' she told me. 'In fact, I was grateful for any notices that weren't negative ones … It was an immensely rewarding experience, not at all awkward − as some may have expected − and I was quite happy.'

Then came an internationally heralded *Hedda Gabler*. Ashcroft played Hedda for comedy and irony, rather than Nordic gloom and doom. Her refreshing interpretation was called definitive and resulted in the King's Gold Medal, bestowed by King Haakon of Norway. Ashcroft took Hedda on tour to Germany and Scandinavia. In 1955 she also toured Europe in *King Lear* and *Much Ado About Nothing*, noting, 'One does feel an added responsibility when performing before an audience for whom English isn't their primary tongue. One's sense of gesture, mood and expression is heightened, and the geographic shifting from one theatre to another also prevents one from taking the theatre or audience for granted.'

In the 1950s, Ashcroft did considerable radio work (though only one television play, for Peter Hall in 1958). Her popularity in various media and lands was capped by the award of DBE in 1956. Suddenly, there was no averting the limelight. Yet she continued to refuse interviews about 'the real Dame Peggy' or to comment on her very private life. Her daughter and son (born in 1941 and 1945, respectively) were off-limits to the press. So were her marriages and divorces: Rupert Hart-Davis, whom she wed in 1929 and divorced in 1931; Komisarjevsky, 1934-7; and barrister – later Lord – Jeremy Hutchinson (the father of her children), whom she married in 1940 and divorced in 1965.

Dame Peggy apprised *Show* magazine: 'It is a flat contradiction in terms to discuss one's private life. The instant one discusses it, it ceases to be a private life.'

When I made so bold as to inquire after her marital alliances with not inconsiderable men – never dreaming to ask why they didn't last longer – she replied, 'It is a trial for a man to be married to an actress. But then, marriage itself is a sort of trial, isn't it? Generally, men prefer ladies with small egos, but also with small accomplishments …'

She added, 'It's my opinion that if an interested party – a fan or journalist – doesn't find ample fare in an actress's career, he will not find it in her off-stage life.'

Ralph Richardson averred, 'Peggy wants to be judged on her career and craft, not her lapses into domesticity.' An anonymous associate stated, 'She is proud of her children and therefore won't talk about them in public, and she is not proud of three divorces and therefore won't talk about them.'

Ever one to take an artistic chance, Dame Peggy returned to the London stage – the Haymarket, via John Gielgud – in Enid Bagnold's controversial *The Chalk Garden* in 1956. (The play had been turned down throughout the West End and was successfully staged in New York before London accepted it.) She played Miss Madrigal opposite Edith Evans's Mrs St Maugham. A governess with a past, Madrigal spent fifteen years in prison as a reprieved murderer; the 1960s screen version featured Deborah Kerr opposite Hayley Mills and Dame Edith as the dowager.

Later that year, 1956, Dame Peggy gambled again. *The Good Woman of Setzuan* at the Royal Court was not only a Marxist parable but the first full-scale staging of a Bertolt Brecht play in English. The actress had a field-day as prostitute-turned-tobacconist Shui Ta, who fabricates and then must impersonate a male cousin in order to keep her humanitarian and capitalist selves separate and thriving. Kenneth Tynan was the more impressed by her male role, marvelling, 'Nothing tougher has been heard since Montgomery last harangued the troops.'

At fifty-plus, she went back to Stratford, once more to revive Rosalind in *As You Like It*. In the West End, she brought the failed Hungarian uprising to life in *Shadow of Heroes*. In Edinburgh, she performed *Portraits of Women*, devised by herself and Ossian Ellis, and in 1958 was in the movies again in the compelling international hit *The Nun's Story*. It starred Audrey Hepburn, with Dame Peggy as Mother Mathilde, directed by Fred Zinnemann. (Ten years passed before her next, even smaller role, as a dotty aunt – 'peripheral women', she called most of the screen characters offered her.)

In 1960, at fifty-two, Dame Peggy took Stratford by storm as Kate the great in *The Taming of the Shrew*. The next year, she joined the Royal Shakespeare Company (formerly the Shakespeare Memorial Theatre Company). It became her permanent artistic home, and in time the ensemble star became one of its directors. During the early 1960s, she helped to revivify England's kings and queens by touring Europe in *The Hollow Crown*. However, after a quantity and quality of Shakespeare and Chekhov, she focused on modern plays for the remaining half of the decade.

An overwhelming role, both in scope and the amount of food the actress had to consume on stage, was Mother in Marguerite Duras's *Days in the Trees*, directed by John Schlesinger in 1966. The *Sunday Times* called the character 'a barmy old bitch' who cossets her gigolo son. In 1968 she returned to the big screen as a grasping aunt in blonde pageboy and spectacles, in Joseph Losey's *Secret Ceremony*. It was a bizarre vehicle for Elizabeth Taylor and Mia Farrow. In 1969 the dame played a barmy mother-in-law in the film *Three Into Two Won't Go*, starring Rod Steiger, Claire Bloom and Judy Geeson. The same year, she was a philanderer's embittered wife in Edward Albee's *A Delicate Balance*, directed by Peter Hall for the RSC at the Aldwych Theatre.

'There is an interlude, in early middle age, when roles of depth and insight are pitifully few for an actress. In one's sixties, closer to old age, the pickings become more plentiful, after the issue of a mid-aged woman's sexuality has been laid to rest – laid to rest in the male [writer's] mind ...'

The 1970s found Dame Peggy as busy as ever, and as experimental. On stage, she had a fleeting role as a famed communist stage director's wife in Günter Grass's *The Plebeians Rehearse the Uprising*, also for the RSC. In *The Lovers of Viorne*, in 1971, she was a schizophrenic but everyday murderer. The *Sunday Telegraph*'s Frank Marcus asseverated, 'If this is not great acting, then I do not know what the term means.'

'Madame Duras presents difficult women,' explained Dame Peggy. 'Her characters are accessible, but not easy. What is easy is seldom worthwhile on either side of the artistic divide.'

Also in 1971, for John Schlesinger, she portrayed Mrs Greville in the bisexual love triangle film *Sunday, Bloody Sunday*, starring Peter Finch and Glenda Jackson. 'Undeniably ahead of its time, ergo not a commercial triumph. But a work of art,' she felt. 'A minor role is not so minor in a picture which stands the test of time and speaks to people's hearts ... Relationships are what actors and spectators seek.'

A 1929 portrait of Peggy Ashcroft.

(*above right*) Ashcroft in the 1932 play *Caesar and Cleopatra*.

(*right*) Dame Peggy won the Oscar for Best Supporting Actress in 1984 for her role in *A Passage to India*. (*Doug McClelland*)

A 1941 portrait of Edith Evans.

Dame Edith in *The Chalk Garden*, 1963. (*Doug McClelland*)

Dame Edith with director Anthony Asquith, *The Importance of Being Earnest*, 1952.

The ensuing year yielded a sizeable role, that of a nearly-dead man's caustic, long-suffering wife in *All Over*, Edward Albee's best play since *Who's Afraid of Virginia Woolf?* It co-starred Angela Lansbury as the man's mistress. The lightweight *Lloyd George Knew My Father* came later in the season. Dame Peggy then alternated Pinter and Ibsen – *John Gabriel Borkman* in 1975, reuniting her with Ralph Richardson and Wendy Hiller – before undergoing Samuel Beckett's *Happy Days* in 1975. At the National Theatre and the Old Vic – and eventually the Lyttelton in 1977 – she enacted the be-hatted Winnie, buried up to her waist and later her neck in earth. The garrulous role begins comically but ends in horror, as Winnie stares into her own dead future.

B.S. Young wrote in the *Financial Times*, 'Peggy Ashcroft is as near perfection as we are likely to see in our time.'

In 1976 she offered *Tribute to the Lady*, the female in question being stage impresario Lilian Baylis. In Tony Richardson's film of Fielding's bawdy *Joseph Andrews*, she was Lady Tattle, and she endured a distinct non-hit in England in the hit Soviet play (in some fifty theatres) *Old World*. Audiences initially materialized to enjoy Ashcroft and Anthony Quayle, but the slight and drab story of a sanatorium director and an elderly patient failed to please. Terry Hands directed for the RSC, one reviewer proclaiming, 'Hands down, a dull evening!'

Two years later, Dame Peggy was on television again, for the first time in seven years. She had the supporting but standout role of Queen Mary in *Edward and Mrs Simpson*, and earned almost unanimous rave reviews. One newspaper declared that she, though not a habituée of the large or small screen, was giving lessons on how to act for the camera. She was the stern queen consort and mum, to the life, gravely intoning lines such as ' What's love compared to duty?' and 'I cannot bear to hear you talk only of your happiness' to her son the king.

Dame Peggy was actually in the centre of James Ivory's

Hullabaloo Over Georgie and Bonnie's Pictures (1978), as Lady Gee in the script by Ruth Prawer Jhabvala. It was her first lead role in a movie.

The 1980s brought still greater acclaim, renown and more challenges. In 1980 she performed at the National in Lillian Hellman's *Watch On the Rhine*, an anti-fascist play written in 1940 with the purpose of pressuring the United States into the Second World War. Also in 1980, she portrayed the Viennese dowager Frau Messner in the excellent BBC telefilm *Caught On a Train*. In 1981 and 1982, at the Royal Shakespeare, then at the Barbican, Dame Peggy was the Countess of Rousillon in *All's Well That Ends Well*. Trevor Nunn's production was hailed as better than the generally less than beloved play, which was further redeemed by the Ashcroftian interpretation of what Shaw considered to be 'the most beautiful old woman's part ever written'.

The moderately frequent TV and film roles peaked in 1984 with two epic Indian-themed productions that at last made Peggy Ashcroft a household name. She played Barbie Batchelor in the globally popular 13-part mini-series, *The Jewel in the Crown*. After the fact, she allowed, 'The coincidental timing of *The Jewel in the Crown* and *A Passage to India* did result in the maximum impact and temporary exposure.'

In David Lean's version of E.M. Forster's book *A Passage to India*, she was Mrs Moore, again contrasting favourably with the starchier and more imperialistic of her countrypeople in India. The (supporting) Academy Award was a foregone conclusion, but she won it in competition with such established screen actresses as Geraldine Page and Glenn Close. Unfortunately, Dame Peggy was too ill to attend the Oscar ceremonies in Hollywood, and Angela Lansbury's acceptance of her Oscar stirred up ill-feeling among many who felt that Ashcroft's Indian co-star Victor Bannerjee – who was in the audience at the time – should have accepted for her. Nor did Ms Lansbury verbalize what Dame Peggy had intended to say: that she wished to thank India and Forster for making it all possible.

Part of the two parallel roles' appeal, admitted the great dame, was 'an opportunity to distinguish between the unthinking British who colonized and brutalized a nation which had its own highly sophisticated culture and religion, and those British who – however misguidedly, for they were also patronizing – sought to do some genuine good'.

As for critics who decried the series' and film's alleged Brit-bashing, she held, 'If we don't re-examine our history and our relationships with other countries, we will be doomed to repeat our mistakes and to cherish in ourselves our least attractive characteristics.'

According to biographer Robert Tanitch, Ashcroft's 'passion for the theatre is matched only by her passion for political causes, and ... her commitment to supporting individuals against tyranny is absolute'. Over the years, she took part in myriad protests, demonstrations, fund-raisers, vigils, petitions and letter-writing campaigns, also perform-ing poetry recitals for Amnesty International and for the magazine *Index On Censorship*, among other *pro bono* activities.

'I prefer not to discuss a particular attempt at illuminating injustice where it exists – that is to say, I prefer to speak about a given case at the time it is occurring, when we are activating on its behalf ... I don't wish to sound like a charity worker or a do-gooder. I merely do what I think must be done, at the moment I feel it should be done.

'If necessary, I discuss my work. But what I do away from acting should not require much comment. Nor should one be over-praised for following one's conscience. I like to think of myself as an individual who cares about others.'

Although illness sometimes intervened, Dame Peggy's credo was 'Keep busy. It uses the mind and energy to positive ends.' After her 1984 double triumph, she worked less but became enshrined as an institution and a survivor.

On 14 June 1991, following a stroke, Dame Peggy Ashcroft passed away at the Royal Free Hospital, probably the last of the truly great stage actresses.

2

Dame Edith Evans

Edith Evans didn't much care for interviews. 'Mind you, I enjoy conversations.' She felt that interviews placed the subject in an awkward position and made the interviewer uncomfortable, 'which makes me uncomfortable'. Though somewhat intimidating – and who wouldn't be, living twinned with the shadow of Lady Bracknell? – the actress was endearing, a gentle and modest soul. Her manner was anything but imperious, and with her ready, genuine smile, she soon put the interviewer at his ease.

With Dame Edith Evans's career, it was a matter of B.B. and A.B. – Before Bracknell and After Bracknell. Her friend, director Bryan Forbes, has said, 'There are few actors of my generation, male or female, who have not at some time or another attempted a parody of Edith's Bracknell voice and delivery.'

Evans's 'great essay in dragonhood', as Forbes called it, was first unleashed on the public in 1939, at London's Globe Theatre. That production of Oscar Wilde's *The Importance of Being Earnest* was produced by and co-starred John Gielgud.

But it was Evans who stole the show, and who would play her part time and again, to perfection, until the play was captured on film in 1952.

By that time, Dame Edith had acted a plethora of roles, nearly all of them on stage, for over four decades. Yet it was her Lady Bracknell with which she became indelibly identified. Upon her death at eighty-eight in 1976, there was scarcely a single obituary, on either side of the Atlantic, that did not mention her indisputably 'best known' and arguably 'best' performance.

In an atypically dark mood, she once claimed, 'I've played her everywhere except on ice and under water … I did play *other* parts, you know!'

To her exasperation, she was known to younger generations primarily as a film actress. Especially as Lady Bracknell. 'I sometimes wonder,' she confided to the author, 'whether I ought to have taken on the screen version. Perhaps I should have stopped with playing her on the stage.'

With time, the immense if comical dignity of Wilde's immortal gorgon became grafted on to Dame Edith's own considerable dignity. To her surprise and dismay, her and Bracknell's Victorian rectitude made her into a figure of fun for certain comedians and many younger fans. During one Academy Awards telecast, Master of Ceremonies Bob Hope joked that the universal new fad of mini-skirts had even been taken up by Edith Evans. When the cameras focused on her, seated in the audience awaiting the verdict on her Best Actress nomination for *The Whisperers*, the elderly Englishwoman's regal bearing made mincemeat of Hope's somewhat tasteless joke.

'The worst affront is when a young person or an interviewer, who should know better, requests me to "do" Bracknell. Of course, they always want to hear me say "*A handbaaag?*" and naturally, I never do.'

With that, she put aside the topic of *Earnest* – Anthony Asquith's film version of which co-starred not Gielgud but

Michael Redgrave – and Lady Bracknell. Her daughter Gwendolyn, a potential gorgon, was essayed by the velvet-voiced Joan Greenwood, who later declared, 'Once in a great while, a role is played so ideally that it is set in stone, as it were. This happened with Dame Edith's Bracknell. The pity of it was that the media didn't permit her to move on to other characterizations. Instead, they kept insisting that she reprise her performance from our film.'

As happened with many long-lived stage stars, even a legendary one like Evans, she in time became best known for her screen roles. Yet her celluloid bow in 1915, at the age of twenty-seven, in *The Welsh Singer*, was not auspicious, and ironically for a performer who became identified with Establishment propriety, she was also seen that year in a movie provocatively titled *Honeymoon For Three*. One more screen effort in 1916, and she abandoned the new medium and returned to her abiding love, the stage.

She realized, 'I couldn't very well succeed in pictures while they were silent, since I think you're aware that my voice is my biggest asset.'

She shied away from the screen until 1948, when, aged sixty, she made her talking movie début. The picture, lavishly produced by Anatole de Grunwald, was *The Queen of Spades*, from Alexander Pushkin's celebrated ghost story – best known until that time for the opera which Tchaikovsky composed in 1890.

'It was a splendid part,' she remembered, 'although not over-long. Oliver Messel created the most wonderfully atmospheric sets ... Visually and psychologically, it is a stunning picture. My part in it was certainly very memorable. Almost as much so as Martita Hunt [as Miss Havisham] in *Great Expectations*.

'As a girl, I doted on ghost stories, and I suppose that's what really attracted me to returning to pictures in *The Queen of Spades*.'

Edith Evans was born in London's faded Pimlico on 8

February 1888. Her father, Ned, was a minor civil servant. Her mother, the ex-Miss Caroline Ellen Foster, was formerly a nurse. The couple had another child, a son, who died at the age of four, when Edith was two. Despite Ned being a genuine Cockney, 'Ned's girl' – as she liked being called in her youth and old age – evolved into a textbook example of eloquent diction and the Queen's English.

'Father never read a book,' she recalled, 'but Mother virtually ate them up. She wanted so much for me to become a lady.'

Thus, at fifteen, when Edith left school, she became an apprentice milliner to a gentleman who made hats for 'ladies of quality', on Buckingham Palace Road. 'If you will forgive the pun, I was never mad about being a hatter, although I did like the pretty colours and fabrics.'

During evening classes at the time, Edith was formally introduced to Shakespeare. 'I began acting out his plays for my pleasure. My lady teacher was very enthusiastic about Shakespeare, and she communicated her enthusiasm to me.'

In 1910 the budding thespian made her stage début as Viola in *Twelfth Night*. The next fourteen years saw Edith serving a long, glittering apprenticeship in the plays of Shakespeare, Shaw and others. 'I took my time learning, and I even learned from my successes.' Several of her successes found her in roles older than her age. 'I suppose in part because of my mien, and in part because of my looks, I was cast as middle-aged in my youth, and as older in my middle-age.

'Although, when I played in Bernard Shaw's *Back to Methuselah* [in 1923], I did *not* play the title character ...'

In 1924 Edith undertook Mrs Millamant in Congreve's *The Way of the World*, a role that she made hers, and which made her nationally famous.

The critic James Agate professed: 'Miss Edith Evans is the most accomplished of living and practising English actresses. Leaving tragedy to Miss Thorndike, she has a wider range than any other artist before the public.'

No actress has since made such an impact as Millamant, the role most closely identified with Edith Evans until Lady Bracknell.

In 1925 the busy actress – who found no time for a honeymoon, even for two! – finally consented to wed George Booth. She had known the handsome ex-ledger clerk since before the Great War, when he had also entertained acting aspirations. But after surviving the war, and once Edith's renown began to mushroom, 'Guy' lost interest in acting and subsequently became a successful oil man. He remained Edith's greatest fan until his death in 1935.

'It isn't necessarily true that a woman today need choose between a career upon the stage and a family life, especially one with children,' explained Dame Edith in 1972, at the Windsor country house of a mutal friend. 'Nowadays, women seem to get whatever they wish, simply by demanding it! It quite amazes me, I can tell you. In my day, women rarely demanded anything. Just to be able to earn one's living was a triumph of the first magnitude, strange as it may now seem.

'But the stage demands so much more time than a career in film or television. As every stage actor knows, one gives up one's private life during the run of a play. Guy suffered for my dedication to the stage … Later on, when I was doing more camera work, I now and again found myself wishing that I had been asked to work in those media during our marriage. Not that it would have been much easier for me, but it certainly would have been easier on poor Guy.'

Her married life was the last topic broached during our interview, arranged through my grandfather, who earlier enabled me to meet Cecil Beaton (it was Sir Cecil who described 'E.E.' as 'a sleeping Boadicea, with those great, hooded eyelids and slightly perplexed lips – but beware when the lady warrior wakens, for she will disarm you with her gentility!'). Dame Edith initially stated, 'I don't think I want to discuss my marriage, because first of all, it is boring to other people, and secondly, it is very private to me.'

A few minutes later, she somewhat relented, and allowed, 'I was happy as a wife. Whether I would have been a happy and doting mother, I do not know, couldn't honestly say. I know it isn't fashionable to eschew parenthood, even now, but truly, the only thing I ever passionately wanted to do was to act. And from what I've seen – which I admit is not much, as I've not chosen to become very familiar with many actresses – most actresses tend to be less than ideal parents.

'After Guy's death in 1935, I threw myself back into my work. Work, and more work. It is the best, the only really reliable, tonic ... What I certainly didn't do, afterwards, was delude myself that a second marriage might some day prove more lasting or somehow more fulfilling for the male partner.

'An actress's sole abiding partner,' she firmly announced, 'is the stage.'

So, in 1935 Edith quietly triumphed on stage as the Nurse in John Gielgud's heralded production of *Romeo and Juliet*, co-starring Gielgud and Laurence Olivier. It was a role she had played before, including a 1934 Katharine Cornell/ Guthrie McClintic production in New York, and would play again (for the last time in 1961). However, 'The dramatic and competitive pleasure of playing opposite John and Larry,' who alternated as Romeo and Mercutio, 'kept me in top form throughout the run.' Most critics concurred that Gielgud was the better Romeo from the neck up, and Olivier from the neck down.

As for the Nurse, Dame Edith noted merrily, 'It's a whale of a part. Even Noël Coward admitted it. Laurence Harvey once asked him why he had never played Shakespeare. Noël had no ready answer. Then Harvey asked whether Noël might ever consider it, and Noël replied that he'd always thought he might do well in *Romeo and Juliet* – as the Nurse!'

There were more stage hits, among them *The Seagull*, Katharina in *The Taming of the Shrew*, *The Importance of Being*

Earnest, Shaw's *The Millionairess* (a tricky part also tackled by Katharine Hepburn, and done on film by Sophia Loren), *Crime and Punishment*, Shaw's *Heartbreak House*, John Van Druten's *Old Acquaintance*, Coward's *Hay Fever*, and even Cleopatra in Shakespeare's *Antony and Cleopatra*.

'On the stage, I could be anyone, most any physical type. Of course the camera demanded otherwise.' Besides which, 'The theatre has always sustained me, in one way or another, and in my career I was always quite happy, if not always entirely satisfied.'

By the 1940s, the actress was a stage institution. In 1946 she was created Dame Edith Evans, and said to be at her artistic peak. But despite *The Queen of Spades*' critical and financial success, she continued to circumvent the screen. And still did, after the warm reception accorded the 1952 film *The Importance of Being Earnest*, from which play she performed highlights of her Lady Bracknell for TV on 22 September 1955, the opening night of commercial television in Great Britain.

'People say I was extremely good in both *Earnest* and *Queen of Spades*, they tell me how they enjoy watching me, and ask whether *I* enjoy watching those particular films? Well, unless one resembles the likes of Greta Garbo, I think the answer is rather obvious. Whenever *I* watch those films, or my scenes, I can't get past my face. My tics, mannerisms, my voice – I'm studying it all, and I become trapped in watching and listening to no one else in the scene.

'This isn't egotism, mind you. It's a form of embarrassment mingled with professional preoccupation; I never stop critiquing myself, trying to improve. I'm in competition with no one but myself … Of course, I do think Anton Walbrook was wonderful as Herman, the army officer, in *Queen of Spades*. I always enjoy watching Anton, a great talent and personality. I remember that we were astounded when the picture's director was fired and we got a new one, and neither of us was consulted, and then everything went on as if nothing unusual had happened! It was shocking, but not unusual in the film industry.

'I of course also enjoyed working with [director] Anthony Asquith in *Earnest*, though I missed the contribution made by John Gielgud, who always sheds his calmness and unselfishness upon an entire cast. Anthony got excellent performances out of all the players, and I relished working with Michael Redgrave, another of our talents, a tremendous one.

'People ask all sorts of questions about my Lady Bracknell and the play, most of which I can answer. What *I* never understood was why it took so long [fifty-seven years] to put such a witty and entertaining play on the screen. To my knowledge, it has always been a consistent crowd-pleaser. I suppose the answer has to do with Mr Wilde's lingering notoriety, and the stuffiness of people who chose to take a dim view of him.'

Hard on the heels of the screen *Earnest* came talk of a film version of *Waters of the Moon*, a 1951 play in which Dame Edith enacted a wealthy socialite opposite Dame Sybil Thorndike. The latter played a taciturn boarding house lodger (in the 1978 West End production, the roles were played by Ingrid Bergman and Dame Wendy Hiller, respectively). The London press made much of the fact that it was the first time two Dames had co-starred in a play. A feud was anticipated, but didn't occur. Even so, the two actresses provided enough on-stage fireworks to keep *Waters* running over a year.

'It wasn't the sort of character most people associated with me,' said Dame Edith, who wore Balmain gowns in the part (Dame Sybil wore tweeds and cardigans). 'It was a glamorous change of pace, and a high point, playing opposite Dame Sybil,' six years her senior, 'whom I had always respected.' Critic Gerald Fay advised readers that 'Anybody intent on getting the full flavour of the acting would need to see the comedy twice, concentrating on a different Dame each time – for how can a person watch simultaneously the extravagant antics of Dame Edith and the glacial repose with which Dame Sybil tries to smother them?'

Ironically, when Hollywood expressed interest in *Waters*, they did so on the basis of casting Evans in Thorndike's part and signing a box office glamourpuss for the central role! Then, as now, the studios only thought in stereotypes, and the project never got off the ground.

The 1950s saw the flowering of Edith Evans's first domestic relationship since Guy's death. Miss Judith E. Wilson had long been her devoted fan and admirer, sending the actress letters and then gifts, that were reciprocated with responses and then invitations to social functions. In 1955, Dame Edith surprised friends and colleagues alike when she moved into a new house with Miss Wilson. Everyone predicted it would not last, for Edith, essentially a loner, had lived alone so long, and become very set in her ways: during her marriage, she had lived more apart from Guy than with him.

Nevertheless, the warm and mutual live-in friendship endured until Judith's death in 1960, which devastated Edith.

In 1958, Edith finally returned to the silver screen as the Mother Superior in the Audrey Hepburn vehicle *The Nun's Story*, directed by Fred Zinnemann. 'Although it was alien to me, the subject matter [a nun's life] was quite compelling. In my opinion, Mr Zinnemann depicted one of the most intense and realistic spiritual stories ever filmed.

'He and Miss Hepburn were wonderful to work with. I know it was a very personal project for her. There was a subplot about the anti-Nazi Resistance in Belgium and Holland, the countries where she was born and grew up, during that period.'

Dame Edith did few film roles until her seventies, but the situation was not entirely of her own choice. On stage, she was still a leading lady. On screen, however, even the right supporting parts were difficult to come by. 'You see, the

Americans didn't know what to make of me after *Earnest*. And until I was old enough to play Reverend Mother or someone's grandmum, there weren't that many offers, even from British picture sources.'

Once she was old enough, she could have followed in the well-paid footsteps of Dame May Whitty or Edna May Oliver as Tinseltown's official portrayer of titled or dotty old ladies. 'Hollywood made a good deal of fuss over me,' she said of *The Nun's Story*, a Warner Brothers production. But leave behind England and the stage? Never. 'Money,' she asseverated, 'is nice in its place, but the idea of money first is the root of all evil.'

After *The Nun's Story* Edith segued into Tony Richardson's *Look Back in Anger*, from John Osborne's seminal play. The 1959 movie starred Richard Burton, Mary Ure (Mrs Osborne) and Claire Bloom. Evans played Ma Tanner, the owner of a shop co-managed by Burton. Her character had only been referred to in the play, and never seen. Richardson and Osborne expanded and tailored her role, fully confident that she could play 'a common old woman'. When certain critics evinced surprise that Dame Edith made a convincing Ma Tanner, she became agitated:

'I'm an *actress*, aren't I? Why do they think I can only play ladies of quality? I know more about the Ma Tanners of this world than I do about the so-called gentry!'

Looking back, she pronounced *Look Back in Anger* 'a good picture, and a significant one, because it ushered in the spate of "angry young man" pictures which helped the British cinema renew itself.

'Of course I knew there was little room for me in most such pictures. Nor in those "swinging London" ones which came into fashion just a few years afterwards.'

Screen acting, she found, was something of a challenge. 'As Bracknell, I had to be larger than life. It was so obviously a filmed *play*. But in naturalistic pictures, I had to scale it all down, you see. The economy of detail was the thing, and directors like Mr Zinnemann and Tony Richardson have a marvellous eye for detail. They recreate an entire world for the camera, where, on the stage, one *suggests* a world.'

Dame Edith explained that her criteria in choosing a play or film varied, depending on the project's elements. With one exception: 'The words. To me, words are very colourful. I can see colours in words. For a time, I even thought I should like to become a writer, once I grew too old to act.'

But the older she got, the more she was in demand, especially on screen. In the 1960s her diverse films included Tony Richardson's *Tom Jones* and Ronald Neame's *The Chalk Garden*. She was Oscar-nominated for Best Supporting Actress for both. *Chalk Garden* starred Deborah Kerr, with Dame Edith as Hayley Mills's confused but well-meaning grandmother, Mrs St Maugham, a role she had created on the stage. The 1956 Enid Bagnold play had been directed by the omnipresent John Gielgud.

The film version, produced by Ross Hunter – best known for his Doris Day comedies – received dreadful reviews, particularly in London, where memory of Evans's electrifying Mrs St Maugham remained strong. Her screen role was cut, and the Bagnold dialogue was Americanized as well as drastically pruned. 'I was very surprised to be up for an Academy Award for it,' she reminisced. 'Of course, I don't like all this voting and campaigning business that goes with awards, and I still hold that if you want to express gratitude to an actor, it's better to give him a dinner than an award.

'But I was flattered by their gesture, in light of the fact that Hollywood paid most of its attention to the picture's younger actresses ...'

For the 1966 *The Whisperers*, Evans was de-glamorized to play Mrs Ross, a part that earned her the Golden Bear for Best Actress at the Berlin Film Festival, the New York Film Critics' Award and the British Academy Award. Bryan Forbes adapted and helmed the story of an elderly woman enduring genteel poverty in Scotland – changed in the movie to England, because the American distributor did not want any 'really weird accents' threatening the film's box office.

When the American press inquired which *method* Dame Edith used to yield such a riveting performance, Forbes offered, 'Her method is that she is simply a great actress.'

He stated that he had expressly adapted the book *Mrs Ross* as a vehicle for the seventy-nine-year-old actress: 'It seemed a tragic waste that nobody had really written a film to make full use of her extraordinary talents.' Evans's idiosyncratic old lady is the heart and nearly the whole of one of the best – and one of the precious few – motion pictures to deal with the elderly. It details her lonely life consisting of trips to the library, a soup kitchen and the National Assistance Board; Mrs Ross lives on a small government pension but insists it is a loan against the 'inheritance' she expects from her deceased father's estate.

At night in her run-down little flat, she hears whispering 'voices' which assuage her craving for company. When her worthless son Charlie (Ronald Fraser) finally does come to visit, it is only to hide stolen money in her closet, which Mrs Ross later finds, believing it to be her long-awaited inheritance ...

When Forbes eventually confessed to Dame Edith how in awe of her he had been when they met in 1952, during the funeral procession of George VI, she expressed disbelief. 'That's something I've never been able to understand. Why anybody should ever be in awe of me, I'm such an *ordinary* person.'

Soon after, Forbes took over direction of *The Madwoman of Chaillot* when John Huston departed over 'creative differences' with its producers. He offered Edith a pivotal role in the movie when Irene Papas also departed, some weeks into filming. The all-star cast boasted Katharine Hepburn, Charles Boyer, Margaret Leighton, Yul Brynner, Giulietta Masina, Danny Kaye, Richard Chamberlain, Nanette Newman (Mrs Forbes), Paul Henreid and Donald Pleasence.

'We shot it in the south of France. It was a colourful but bizarre story, about greed versus nostalgia, I think. The cast was like a miniature United Nations. I believe there was even a Russian [Oscar Homolka], and of course I replaced a Greek actress, and they had to reshoot the scenes in which my character and the rest of the cast appeared together. The set was bristling with energy and pressure, but I found the climate and my co-workers quite charming.'

When Kate Hepburn found out Dame Edith was staying at a hotel, she invited her to move into the rented villa she was sharing with her companion Phyllis Wilbourn. The Englishwoman politely declined, then told her director she'd done so because 'Miss Hepburn goes to bed at half past seven!'

She later revealed, 'Poor Bryan was in rather an uncomfortable position, because in that particular Oscar derby [1967], I was up for Best Actress against his other star,' nominated for *Guess Who's Coming to Dinner*. Directing both actresses in their numerous scenes together, Forbes had to feign impartiality, but subsequently confessed that he had been rooting for Evans (Hepburn won, her second of four statuettes).

Madwoman was not a success for anyone concerned. Forbes attributed this to the difficulty of transferring brilliant writing (by Giraudoux) and sheer theatricality to the screen (as happened with *The Chalk Garden*). Dame Edith noted, 'In some of the stills I've seen from that picture, I look more than usually bewildered. I don't think it's entirely in character, or because of the glasses I wore. I think several of us *were* at times bewildered!'

'There is one thing which most actresses will never admit,' declared Dame Edith in an unflinching assessment of her later screen career. 'It has nothing to do with looks. As a girl, I was told I was plain; I almost believed it, but I wasn't. As an actress, I never had to look in a mirror to see my warts. And as a woman, I knew I was not beautiful, but I had *something* ... What most distinctive actors, female or male, won't admit to is that there inevitably comes a point when you begin to parody yourself.

'This is a danger for the dedicated actor, something to be

avoided. If it can be, for the director – if he's not a very good or conscientious director – may encourage such parodying. They tell you it's "commercial", and what the public expects.

'I could have spent more time before the cameras parodying Bracknell or whatever image they had of me. But once I saw what they wanted, I began to pull back. They wanted me to perform, but to stop acting.'

After *Madwoman*, Dame Edith did fewer film roles, most of them one-dimensional and in projects of varying quality. She did audience-pleasing *grande dame* turns in *Fitzwilly* with Dick Van Dyke and *Prudence and the Pill* with Deborah Kerr and David Niven. 'Unfortunately, to a Hollywood studio, *character* usually meant putting a large, impressive hat on my head, rather than writing some good lines for me to speak. In *Prudence*, my role was very abbreviated, since the plot had to do with sex and the birth control pill, and so I was the grandmotherly comic relief, you see. Still, it had a fine cast. That excuses a lot.'

The actress then took on two Dickens classics, *David Copperfield* (made for American television but released in UK cinemas) and *Scrooge*, a 1970 musical version of *A Christmas Carol*, starring Albert Finney; Dame Edith played the Ghost of Christmas Past.

'Some of my contemporaries look down upon television and film adaptations of Shakespeare or Dickens and so on. But the fact is that very few young people would otherwise be familiar with these works, or be led to read them or to see them acted out upon the stage.'

Dame Edith also participated in Leon Uris's *QB VII* in 1974, one of the first TV mini-series, depicting some of the horror of the Holocaust. 'Well, again, some people think we do too much "rehashing", as they say, of the last great war. I incline to think that the Nazis don't make a very good theme for the stage. However, on television and sometimes in film, it's very effective. The story can be most compelling, with good entertainment value, and even so teach audiences what really happened, and in so doing, try to ensure that it never happens again.'

She also co-starred in mindless entertainments like *The Slipper and the Rose* – a Cinderella musical remake – and self-styled comedies like the cheerfully dreadful *Crooks and Coronets*, its title vainly invoking the comedy classic *Kind Hearts and Coronets* (its American title was actually *Sophie's Place*, and it co-starred Telly Savalas).

'*Crooks and Coronets* was somewhat more fun to do than to watch. I admit it. It did make a good point, though: I played a lady with a big manor who cannot continue to maintain it, given her financial circumstances. Then an American enters the picture, as it were, and it becomes a comedy. Well,' she coughed discreetly, 'one of those transatlantic comedies ...'

By this time, the actress had all but given up the stage. Its physical requirements proved too taxing, and unlike older male stage stars, she had a small choice of roles. 'That's because in the old days, almost all the writers were men, and today's female writers write about *young* women.' As for rumours that she had trouble memorizing her lines, 'When we were shooting *Scrooge*, I was eighty-one. The only trouble I had with my part was understanding who I was. How can a director explain a *ghost?*

'So it was up to me to pattern her after somebody, and once I chose my old Auntie, I sailed right through.'

Dame Edith stated with a smile that certain directors had preconceived notions about her being difficult. 'Yet I have rarely made a fuss, and have always welcomed direction. I want good direction, and I expect it ... People outside the business imagine that I must be like the characters I've played, particularly in film. But everyone in the business who's worked with me realizes that I'm really rather a marshmallow!'

Asked to compare British and American directors, she found, 'I cannot. There are no real differences, nationality-wise. Only personality-wise. A good, considerate, communicative director transcends all boundaries.' Regarding the differences between British and American actors, she mock-warned, '*That* I could not say. I might be prejudiced, you see.'

Dame Edith's last role, in 1976, was in the movie *Nasty Habits*. She was a nun again, in the Watergate spoof by Muriel Spark – from her novel *The Abbess of Crewe* – starring Glenda Jackson. 'It's a marvellous idea,' she told *Photoplay*. 'Glenda plays Nixon, and I believe Sandy Dennis is John Dean, and a lovely blonde actress [Susan Penhaligon] is the McGovern character … I have no idea whether it will go over with the public.' Somehow, it didn't.

The woman often labelled 'the last great classical English actress' did finally reconcile her film career with her stage one. In her eighties, she conceded, 'It all comes together, in the end. All that really matters, anyway, is the work, and the fact of the work – going out and being with the others, getting to play people far more exciting than oneself.

'I've been asked what I would have been if I hadn't become an actress. That's rather like asking what sort of person I'd have become if I'd been born a man! At the time when I began to act, this was one of very few professions open to women. I was lucky that I wanted to succeed at this profession. I certainly wouldn't have taken on a career for a career's sake. I would only want to do something I could do well.

'By and large, my life has been very full and privileged. If at times I've been misunderstood or even limited, so be it. What right has Ned's girl to complain? I wouldn't dare – I've been far too fortunate!'

3

Hermione Gingold

*'Giving interviews is my hobby,' cooed Hermione Gingold
one spring afternoon in New York City in 1984. 'If I
weren't so flamboyantly articulate, most Americans
wouldn't know me.' She became a household face in the
US via talk shows, starting with Jack Paar. She was
already familiar from her memorable turns in films like*
Gigi, The Music Man *and* Bell, Book and Candle. *'I
haven't yet become a household name. In fact, I've been
publicly introduced as everything from Hermione Gielgud
to Hermoganie Gingold to Herman Gingold!'*

In 1988 Hollywood columnist Hank Grant wrote,
'Brothers David and Robert Joseph of Glasgow,
Scotland, couldn't have been more surprised that
grandmother Hermione Gingold had left them $150,000 in
her will. They hadn't even met her, except briefly as babies,
because their father Leslie Joseph was one of two sons
"abandoned" by Hermione after her marriage to publisher
Michael Joseph went sour.'

Gingold, who died in the spring of 1987, at eighty-nine,
told various interviewers, 'I was never maternal, even after I
became a *mater*. I'm sorry, but there you are. I've never liked

children, and having a few didn't change my mind.'

Nor was she mad about husbands, of whom she had a couple; the second was Eric Maschwitz, who once worked at the publishing firm of Hutchinson. 'My husbands did leave me something to remember them by – a love of good books. I wrote two of my own.' They included the satirical *Sirens Should Be Seen and Not Heard*. Her third and final book was the posthumously published autobiography, *How To Grow Old Disgracefully*.

La Gingold informed me, 'My first husband tried to kill me ... I mistakenly married for business, not romance, and when I fell in love with romantic Eric, Joseph found out, and beat me black and blue. Then he took out a razor, waved it at me and threatened murder – mine! He was the sort of personality that had I shown I was frightened, he would have. He wanted a weak wife, but loathed women who frightened easily.

'So I hollered back at him – my best-ever performance as an actress – "Don't be silly!" and he slammed his way out and locked the door. I escaped through the window and took a ferry, then a train, back to London.'

In London she had been born Hermione Ferdinanda Gingold in 1897. 'If that name wasn't a handicap, I don't know what is.' The moniker was chosen by her mother. 'She had a second child, my sister. She must have been in a more merciful mood, for she named her Margaret ...' As a performer, Hermione came to appreciate her name, because 'It's so long on a marquee that there isn't room for another actor's beside mine.'

Her father was a stockbroker – 'and Mother had a lot of time on her hands too'. She admitted, 'You could write the feelings of love I had for my mother on the head of a pin ... Her primary ambition was to have a nervous breakdown.'

Kate was scandalized when her daughter opted for acting. 'My mother once told my father that she wouldn't entertain a certain woman in their house, because the woman in question dyed her hair ... Mother's sister Dolly used to write poetry, so Mama disapprovingly called her "your Aunt Bohemia".'

While relishing strawberries and cream at the Algonquin, Gingold stated, 'I'm not the only colourful member of my family. My mother was dull and terribly decent, but she was one of ten sisters. Seven of them were renowned for their beauty – Mama was one of the other three ... My Aunt Gertie was beautiful, with a beautiful singing voice. She had a daughter named Patricia, who grew up and had an affair with my second husband.'

On a talk show, the comedienne was asked if her second husband was still alive? She drawled in the basso profundo once described as a mixture of 'powdered glass in dark syrup', '*That* is a matter of opinion.'

Hermione's yen for showbiz was viewed more kindly by her father James, 'a wildly extravagant man who loved handsome shoes, silk pyjamas and the best of everything. He went through three fortunes, one of which he made himself. In later years he completely reformed and became a Buddhist and my role model.'

James's sister Helene was Hermione's early role model. 'She was so theatrical, she might as well have been in the theatre. She was six feet tall, and known as Aunt Baby. She was a baroness; how she became one had something sexy to do with the King of Greece. She would hire a box and take my sister and me to theatre matinées. She claimed she was a colonel of a Greek regiment, and would wear a rather startling uniform. People stared, and she would remark, "You'd think they'd never seen a woman in uniform before." Which of course they hadn't!

'Other times at the theatre, in the evenings, she would wear a Greek tunic à la Isadora Duncan and grapes in her hair. Then people would stare at her and say things like, "She must be advertising something." '

As a child, Hermione took up singing, piano and fencing lessons, and studied acting with 'the great Rosina Filippi'. Miss Filippi arranged for her pupil to audition for Sir

Herbert Beerbohm Tree at His Majesty's Theatre when she was ten. 'I sang a grown-up song called 'Two Eyes of Grey', and got the part of a herald in *Pinkie and the Fairies*. I had no idea how humble I really should have been, for the cast included Ellen Terry, Mrs Patrick Campbell, Marie Lohr and Lady Tree.

'By that time, the great Ellen Terry was nearly blind. When she first saw me in makeup, she declared that my makeup was terrible. I thought, "How can she tell?" She took me to her dressing room – a great honour – and I kept hoping she wouldn't mistakenly poke my eye out while she redid my makeup.'

Pinkie was a hit, and so was little Hermione with W. Graham Robertson, the play's author. He sent her red roses and asked if he could paint a portrait of her in her heraldic costume? 'I wrote him a thank-you note beginning "Dear Sir". Mama was horrified. She warned me that only tradespeople began letters with "Dear Sir". Then she almost had her longed-for breakdown when she found out I was wanted as an artist's model! So that put an end to my modelling career before it started.'

Hermione was later made Pinkie's understudy, and when the play went on tour in 1909 she was tapped for the star spot. 'My Aunt Judy went on tour with me as chaperone, and my mother waited to have a nervous breakdown until I returned home – an audience of both her daughters was twice as satisfying as a performance for my little sister alone.'

For a time, Hermione had to leave the stage and concentrate on her education, via a governess and tutors. She did occasional theatricals, and was in demand: 'When I was a baby, Mama told me, people would peer into my pram and say, "What an ugly baby." Then I blossomed into a beautiful blonde child. Of course with adulthood I returned to complete ugliness again, though I was always attractive, especially to men.'

At the Savoy Theatre, she understudied the leading child

in *Where the Rainbow Ends*. Little Noël Coward had five lines as a pageboy named William. 'People were astonished by him, because he acted just like an adult. Even then, I could see he would go far ... A few times, he came to tea, but one time we both jumped up and down on the furniture, and my mother was furious. She said, "You are never to ask that boy to tea again. He has no manners, and will never amount to anything."

'Noël and I were very friendly as children. However, as adults we drifted apart, because by then we each needed to be the complete centre of attention.'

Prior to the First World War, Hermione played a few Shakespearian roles at the Old Vic and elsewhere. In *Troilus and Cressida* she was Cassandra. 'When we met for the first rehearsal, in walked a figure in a mackintosh and a homburg. I thought it might be the wardrobe mistress, but it was Edith Evans. She was playing the beautiful Cressida, although her face didn't seem to fit properly. I thought she'd have to use a lot of makeup, but how wrong I was. Miss Evans just sat in front of the mirror and said, "I'm beautiful, I'm beautiful," and she was.'

In *The Merchant of Venice*, 1914, Hermione played Jessica. Her first and last interview with Old Vic despot Lilian Baylis was a daunting experience:

' "Hermione!" she said, "that wig of yours is an insult to the audience. Get rid of it."

' "But Miss Baylis," I whimpered, "it's not a wig, it's my own hair!"

' "I don't care," she said, banging the desk with her fist, "it goes back to the wigmaker tomorrow!"

' "Yes, Miss Baylis," I said. No one argued with her. Actors who asked her for a rise were told, "I'll ask God, dear." Then she would shut her eyes, pray silently and finally say, "I'm sorry, dear. God says no." '

The war interrupted Hermione's career but yielded marriage and pregnancy. 'My mother was thrilled and said I would love the baby the moment I saw it. As always, she was wrong.' The frustrated actress went on 'some very tatty tours ... Certain young players become a *tour de force*, but most are forced to tour.' Then came a second son, 'and soon after that, I got pregnant again and began haemorrhaging. I nearly died, and swore that if I survived, I would leave Joseph.

'Mama kept pleading for me to give up the theatre and become just a mother. She tried to tempt me by saying, "Just think, if you quit acting, you could devote yourself to learning the harp or bowling." '

With a second, less domineering husband, Hermione returned to the West End. In 1921 'I was Liza in *If* and the elderly Maudie in *The Dippers* [1922]. Tatty parts, but I was in the theatre again, earning money, and bowling balls never even entered my mind. Although years later, as a lavish party-giver, I considered writing a book titled *Balls I Have Held*.'

Husband Eric started writing scripts which he sold to the BBC under the pseudonym Holt Marvell. One was a musical called *Goodnight, Vienna*. After its radio broadcast, director Herbert Wilcox bought the screen rights for £200; in 1932 it became the first British talking musical, starring Wilcox's wife Anna Neagle. 'The film was a rollicking success, but Eric wasn't too sad about the deal, because the musical play had a long West End run and went out on several tours.'

Hermione shed Eric when she found out he was sleeping around. But thanks to him, she had got her foot in the door and was performing in radio dramas – 'more suitable for my face'. Two productions she co-starred in were considered radio landmarks: *Carnival*, directed by John Gielgud's brother Val – 'It used two orchestras, which reminds me, "wireless" was quite a misnomer, for living rooms equipped with radio had to sport quite an array of cables, leads and wires, etc' – and *Kaleidoscope*, broadcast in 1929. 'I played the wife, a thankless role that I would be shunning for the rest of my real life!'

On radio, Gingold went on to play everything from a

bullfrog ('They didn't have a sound effects library yet') to the piano. She also began writing BBC plays, the most popular of which was *Tickets, Please*, about a stranded theatrical troupe that must perform at a railway station to earn their tickets home.

'Eventually I was to play in something by Jean Cocteau, very avant-garde – I played a telegram. Unfortunately, it also included a whip and a washboard, and when the BBC general manager came in during rehearsals, he felt we were *too* avant-garde to go out on the air, so that wasn't that.'

BBC censorship also invaded a play in which Hermione enacted a cat. 'I was going to say, "The cat sat in the tree and spat defiance." But a memo warned us that the audience might take offence at the word "spat", so I had to change it to "hissed defiance".' Yet the actress-writer *was* able to present a character of her own invention named Mrs Pullpleasure ... Her most famous radio character was the long-running Mrs Doom from *Mrs Doom's Diary*, a show similar in tone to the American TV series *The Addams Family* or *The Munsters*.

'Radio was marvellous, for it was such a big thing then. It gave me national exposure, after a fashion, and allowed me to sharpen my skills as a voice and a writer. But I was too much of an egotist not to be seen, and at times I literally itched to return to the stage, legitimate or otherwise.'

Throughout the 1920s, Hermione tried to do dramatic plays but typically wound up an understudy. 'Thank heaven for the Gate, just down the road from my flat. This was the early 1930s, and it was a tiny theatre club, and therefore not bound by the usual censorship, else it could never have put on O'Neill's *Desire Under the Elms* or Lillian Hellman's *The Children's Hour*.' At the Gate, she worked with Flora Robson – 'very business-like, but sensitive, a dramatic *tour de force*' – and Elsa Lanchster – 'far more versatile than people remember, but she chose to hide her bushel under Charles Laughton's great big light.'

The Gate Theatre, which paid each player three pounds a week, helped launch future film stars such as Vivien Leigh, James Mason and Michael Wilding. 'I tried to approximate Vivien's beauty but was told my expression looked as if I had a toothache … I met one of my best friends at the Gate, Robert Helpmann … I remember Elsa once played Little Lord Fauntleroy to great effect.' Then the Gate closed down, until 1939.

'I was living with a sexy gentleman friend and scrounging for work. A few theatrical producers were interested, but not in a professional way. They would invite me to their offices at night, for a whisky and sofa. Yes, *sofa*. One of them had the cheek to nickname me Hormone Gingold!'

Meanwhile, Eric Maschwitz was going from strength to strength. He wrote the song 'These Foolish Things Remind Me of You', 'which he led me to believe he'd written about me. Then I found out he'd said the same thing to any number of actresses.' He became rich via royalties from 'A Nightingale Sang in Berkeley Square', 'Room Five Hundred and Four', etc. After their divorce, when Gingold had established herself as a celebrity, she bumped into her ex at a Buckingham Palace garden party:

'He was rolling in money, so I strolled up to him and said, "Eric, darling, what about some alimony?"

' "Oh, no," he insisted. "I could never take money from a woman." '

In 1936 Gingold made her screen début in *Someone at the Door*. Her pre-war films amounted to three, with only one during the 1940s – *The Butler's Dilemma* – before she was rediscovered for movies in the 1950s. 'My problem was trying to show producers and the public what I did best. Yet even I wasn't sure what that was! All I knew was, comedy was my forte … I was too old for an ingénue and too much of a dragon to be Anna Neagle. I once joked that had she played Blanche Dubois, the vehicle would have been re-titled *A Streetcar Named Respectability*.'

Nineteen-thirty-nine was Hermione's turning point. She was in *The Gate Revue*, which led to *Swinging the Gate*. 'As I went along, things centred on me more and more. I was becoming known as a sublime revue artiste and ad-libber! I also did much of my own best material, as I always loved to lampoon things.' *Sky High* (1942), which lasted seven months, led to the fabled revue *Sweet and Low* (1943). 'At last, a show that depended entirely on me, and in which *I* could star!'

There were three *Sweet and Low* revues, including the sequels *Sweeter and Lower* and *Sweetest and Lowest*. They lasted three years, a record beaten only by *Chu-Chin-Chow*. The satirical revues were ahead of their time and barely got past the Lord Chamberlain (the censor). For example, the 'Cello' sketch presented la Gingold as an outrageously bow-legged cellist: 'They don't come to hear me play, they come to see me walk away.' She would later repeat it on Ed Sullivan. (The sketch was inspired by a real-life incident in which a conductor berated his cellists, 'Ladies, you have the most beautiful instrument in the world between your legs, and all you can do is scratch it.')

Other objects spoofed included Wagnerian warrior-maidens – 'In the Rhine I was thrust, now I've rust on me bust' – the poisonous Borgias – 'Isn't it sickening, we've run out of strychnine' – Victorian ladies and their carriages – 'That filly of fable, adorable Mabel, the horse with the hansom behind' – and Robert Helpmann's Freudian interpretation of Hamlet.

The *farceuse* also ribbed famous personalities: 'Look who Errol Flynn's with – that will cause a sensation!' 'But Hermione, he's alone.' 'That's what I mean.' Or, 'Oh, look, there's Florence Desmond doing an imitation of John Gielgud. Oh, no, it *is* John Gielgud.' 'I was like Joan Rivers, but long before her. In those pre-television days, it was thought very daring of us to poke fun at the stars by name.'

Thus she was labelled 'England's debunker-in-chief.'

She reminisced, 'Those were probably the best years of

my life. The nights were sweet, and my mornings were deliciously low, for I had scads of affairs with soldiers, and American servicemen were mad about me ... Our shows became both famous and notorious, and I received as much fan mail as when I was in Hollywood. The most ridiculous fan letter I got was one American's request, "Dear Sir or Madam, Please could you send me a signed photo?" Which I did right away. He sent back a thank-you note which said, "Dear Sir, Thank you for the signed photograph."

'The GIs would bring me things that were impossible for civilians to obtain, such as chocolate, butter, eggs and false eyelashes.'

When the shows ended in 1946, they had played to 800,000 people. 'I did 1,676 performances, and my dresser Kitty never missed one of my 17,010 changes. I had about sixteen changes per show ... The last night of *Sweetest and Lowest* was the end of an era. One GI flew three thousand miles from Boston to see it, and over fifty fans queued up all night. Police were summoned to handle the crowds, and some fans claimed to have seen our revue thirty, forty, even fifty times. I ordered food and drink for the loyal fans who'd queued overnight. After the curtain came down, I sobbed for hours.'

With three solid years of revue behind her, Hermione was ready for a change. She turned an ear towards Hollywood but found she was deemed too eccentric to elicit much interest. 'So I did another revue – rather a case of *déjà-revue* – called *Slings and Arrows* [1948]. But having tasted stardom in the *Sweet and Lows*, I wanted something more – preferably to be knighted! After all, I was almost old enough. But thanks to an indiscreet member of the press, we blew my chance.

'I'd been invited to a garden party at the Prime Minister's – No. 10 Downing Street, which has a large garden behind it. As I departed, a journalist casually inquired what I thought of the party. I said, "I loved it, but the cakes were stale," which they were. The next day, splashed all over the papers was "Hermione Gingold Found Downing Street Cakes Stale." So much for my OBE, I thought, let alone a DBE!

'That's when I started giving serious thought to moving across the sea and getting a fresh start. I might never have done it, however, had I known that I would only be allowed to leave Britain with just five pounds on me.'

Before settling in America, Hermione tried some domestic media. 'I did one classy film, *The Pickwick Papers* [1952], then slipped way down the pole into something called *Cosh Boy* [*The Slasher* in the US] that same year. Joan Collins was in it, and I played her daughter – or the other way round. But despite, or because of, her over-protective father, we did get along, and being both Jewish, had plenty to talk about!'

The 1953 movie *Our Girl Friday* was re-titled *The Adventures of Sadie* for the American market and was Hermione's last till 1956 and Hollywood: 'With *Around the World in 80 Days*, I finally appeared in a major motion picture. Unfortunately, it somewhat discouraged me, as I couldn't help but think that the bigger the picture, the smaller my role in it would be.'

In 1949 she co-starred with her old sparring partner Hermione Baddeley in Noël Coward's *Fallen Angels*. The revival became a huge hit and was her first stage play in seven years. 'I wanted again to sustain a character through three acts. I also wanted top billing, and would *not* take second place. A compromise was reached – we both got top billing, and the advertisement/poster reflected this.' It was a photo of the two Hermiones, head by head, one facing north, the other south, and 'It was turned upside-down every other night [at the theatre], except that there really was no 'upside-down' to it.'

Critic Robert Gerard wrote, 'These lovable gargoyles burlesque Coward's somewhat old-fashioned play, but the spectators love it. The ladies compete fiercely for laughs – their clashes and *faux-pas* should set the box office humming.' Gingold recalled that Coward was not amused, until he got the good news from the ticket-vendors. The play ran over a year.

'Baddeley and I must have done something right, for when *Fallen Arches* – I mean *Angels* – was revived as a straight play with Constance Cummings it was no hit. And when Baddeley redid it in America with Joan Blondell, it opened and closed so quickly it created a vacuum.'

The two namesakes had co-starred in the revues *Rise Above It* and *Sky High*. 'It irritated me no end that we were often mistaken for sisters or lumped together as if we were a duet … She'd said some nasty things about me, and I retaliated in kind and even pretended she was my mother, though she *may* have been a few years my junior.' After *Fallen Angels*, when Baddeley did a play called *Diary of a Nobody*, Gingold declared, 'I think she wrote it herself.'

When the pair both ended up living in America, Baddeley situated herself on the West Coast and advised Gingold to remain on the East Coast because 'This country's barely big enough for the both of us, sister!'

By the mid 1950s, Hermione Sr was in America to stay. But disappointment followed disappointment. 'My big ambition was to do a revue – what I did best, according to my public – on Broadway.' It never happened, thanks partly to a bad musical accompanist at the auditions which the newcomer was forced to give in New York. 'Then I did a record album of my best revue numbers. Decades on, it became a classic, but when it first came out, it was coolly received … And to my amazement, I discovered that winter in New York is actually colder than in London!'

Hermione's friend Beatrice Straight decided to co-produce a play for her, *Lilly Henry*. She moved into an apartment which Straight (an Oscar-winner for *Network*, 1976) had found for her, but the heating kept breaking down, and the play's last act never jelled, so the project was finally called off. As was a promising musical play by Sandy Wilson (*The Boyfriend*) based on Cecil Beaton's *My Royal Past*:

Hermione Gingold and feathered friends in *Promise Her Anything*, 1965. (*Doug McClelland*)

La Gingold with Terry-Thomas in *Rocket to the Moon* (US title: *Those Fantastic Flying Fools*), 1967. (*Doug McClelland*)

Joan Greenwood with Alec Guinness in *The Man in the White Suit*, 1951.

Greenwood in a 1956 telefilm of Shaw's *Man & Superman*.

Greenwood, Michael Redgrave and Michael Denison in *The Importance of Being Earnest*, 1952.

'Anita Loos wanted to put it on, and I would have starred with Jeanette MacDonald … During the read-through, Mac-Donald got stony silences from the assembled company where she should have got laughs. It was a brilliant musical comedy, but she had little or no sense of humour, and resented that I was getting laughs. So she withdrew, and since I wasn't a big enough name in America and they couldn't find a star to replace the leaden Iron Butterfly, it was all scrapped. So sad.

'*Au fond*, I'm like that song Barbra Streisand sang in *Funny Girl* – "I'm the greatest star, but no one knows it." '

Boris Karloff, a fan of Gingold's, wanted to do a revue with her. They finally found the time during the 1960s. He favoured the title 'The Monster and I', while she preferred 'I and the Monster' (wags said the first title indicated that Hermione had achieved top-billing), but then they both received movie offers and permanently postponed the revue.

'I zigzagged between America and Europe, trying to locate lasting success … In 1951 I'd made my American début at Cambridge, Massachusetts, in a revue called *It's About Time*. I thought it would be better than nothing, and it was. Much better, for my ploy worked – John Murray Anderson accepted my invitation to come see me, he liked what he saw, and cast me in a Broadway show with the dubious title *John Murray Anderson's Almanac* (1953). It took a long time to prepare, so in the interim I followed Marlene Dietrich to the Café de Paris to do cabaret in London.'

Described by its producer as 'a musical harlequinade', *Almanac* was a big hit and made Gingold a Broadway star. Her co-stars included Billy DeWolfe, Polly Bergen, Cyril Ritch-ard, Harry Belafonte and Orson Bean. Hermione's visitors' book was signed by everyone from Marilyn Monroe to Yehudi Menuhin. She explained, 'My American success came not a moment too soon. One day on Park Avenue I was stopped by an Englishwoman. She pointed at me – most un-English behaviour! – and demanded, "You know how I recognized you? By your *face*." I congratulated her, then she asked me,

"Didn't you used to be Hermione Gingold?" '

The revue earned its star a Donaldson Award for the best musical comedy début and might have run indefinitely if not for Anderson's sudden death. 'We closed down ... I was out of work again, and my next revue, *Sticks and Bones* [1956], wasn't a hit, so out of desperation I travelled to Los Angeles to appear in *The Sleeping Prince* [1956]; I was the prince's mother. They just loved to think of me as a mother ...'

Television made Gingold known to the average American. Her multi-media career included generous dollops of TV. Two of her early shows were *She Stoops to Conquer* with Michael Redgrave on *Omnibus Playhouse* and *Toast of the Town*. *Pageant* magazine estimated that these programmes were seen by a combined fifty million Americans, 'which astounded me, when I thought that it took three years of back-breaking work for me to be seen by 800,000 people on a London stage! I *love* telly!'

As always, the sixty-ish star wanted to work a lot. 'I require people. Unlike Garbo, I practically never "vant to be a-lone".' In 1957 and 1958 she attempted summer stock. 'We don't have it in England, and to me it sounded like a recipe for a wonderful soup – but I nearly landed in the potage!' She performed both summers in *Fallen Angels*, but chose there-after to stick to 'a nice, comfortable theatre made of real bricks, with real running water and a real staff of grown-up people.'

Nineteen-fifty-eight was perhaps the acme of Gingold's career, with her two best screen roles in her two most cherished films. In *Gigi* she was the title character's (Leslie Caron's) grandmother, Mamita Alvarez. 'Vincente Minnelli was a difficult director to work for, but a perfectionist, and it paid off handsomely. He did confuse me by insisting that I use my own accent, even though I was playing a Frenchwoman and all the stars – Leslie, Louis Jourdan, Maurice Chevalier – had French accents. I'd so been looking forward to acting and sounding French!'

Gingold's duet with Chevalier, the bittersweet 'I Remember It Well,' became a classic.

In *Bell, Book and Candle*, from John Van Druten's play, she was an imperious witch named Mrs De Passe, 'a sort of satanic lady-in-waiting ... It was fun, and Kim Novak was charming and considerate – not typical of young stars.'

But the two triumphs did not lead to a steady movie career. Her next role would be in 1961 in *The Naked Edge*, Gary Cooper's final picture. In 1959 Hermione entertained high hopes for a musical stage version of *Pride and Prejudice*. Renamed *First Impressions*, it co-starred Farley Granger and Polly Bergen. Gingold had two solo numbers, and Kenneth Tynan felt, '[Her] Mrs Bennet is no longer the vague, fussy, provincial matchmaker of Jane Austen's imagination, but a bubbling dragoness fully capable of withering her husband with a single fire-darting glare.

'Needless to say, most of what Miss Gingold does is strangely hilarious. No actor commands a more purposeful leer, and in nobody's mouth do vowels more acidly curdle.'

A patriot to the end – she declined to apply for American citizenship – Hermione opined, 'Abe Burrows was the wrong director for that show ... I think it could have been a success if we'd had an English director.'

Another non-hit was the revue *From A to Z*, which never reached Broadway despite material by Jerry Herman and Woody Allen. It was Gingold's last revue, partially offset by the critical and popular acclaim accorded *The Music Man* (1961). 'I played Eulalie Shinn, the mayor's wife, and one of my songs was deuced difficult. "Pick a Little, Talk a Little, Chirp Chirp Chirp, Talk a Lot, Pick a Little More." And that was just the title!

'At the end of each verse, I boomed out "Balzac", which always got a laugh, and became a catchword at the studio.'

In 1962 Gingold joined forces with Judy Garland for the animated feature *Gay Purr-ee*. They played Persian cats. In 1964 she reteamed with Maurice Chevalier in *I'd*

Rather Be Rich, a showcase for Sandra Dee and Andy Williams. Hermione played an eagle-eyed nurse minding mischievous Maurice. In 1965 she was a vaudevillian-turned-landlady in the Leslie Caron/Warren Beatty-starrer *Promise Her Anything.*

'My subsequent efforts were nothing to write home about, but they were harmless fun,' for instance *Munster, Go Home!* (1966) and *Rocket to the Moon* (1967; *Those Fantastic Flying Fools* in the US).

'As a guest star, I did scads of TV shows, and was often chagrined to discover I was seldom hired for my acting ability, but rather for my personality. Oh, well. I've had at least as much fun as any teary tragedienne.'

Through the 1960s and 1970s, Hermione focused on the stage, touring frequently and sometimes stepping in for other actresses, as when she replaced Molly Picon as Clara Weiss in *Milk and Honey* (1962) and took over as Madame Rosepettle from Jo Van Fleet in *Oh, Dad, Poor Dad, Mama's Hung You in the Closet and I'm Feeling So Sad* (1963). 'Rosepettle was my *tour de force*, my favourite of my dramatic roles, although I yearned to star in *Hamlet*. It's still possible. Sarah Bernhardt played him when she was seventy-five and had a wooden leg!'

Though she took an occasional play to London, Hermione preferred to dwell in New York. 'The London I knew was fast losing its elegance, and besides, as a foreigner in America, I could stand out more readily. Americans are awed by the English. Me, I'm just plain English and odd!'

More stage ensued, including *Charley's Aunt* in Princeton, *Dumas and Son* in LA, and in 1970 Noël Coward's *Fallen Angels* and *Fumed Oak* in South Africa, directed by their star actress. Unexpectedly, she was made a Dame of the Knights of Malta: 'England has never seen fit to give me a British Damehood, which doesn't surprise me. But I was delighted to become a Maltese Dame, and was told I'm entitled to call myself Dame Hermione. I don't do it, but I'm awfully proud of that honour.'

Her final movie role was in *Garbo Talks* (1984) – a forgetful actress – and her last stage turn was *Side By Side By Sondheim* (1977). But her last hurrah was the four years she spent as Madame Armfeldt, the leading lady's baroque mother in Stephen Sondheim's musical *A Little Night Music* (1973). Earning the role required doing her first audition in three decades:

'Hal Prince, the director, said I was superb. But he wasn't convinced I could age enough to play a seventy-four-year-old woman. I told him, "I *am* a seventy-four-year-old woman!" ' (She was seventy-five.) On Broadway, she played the rich ex-courtesan for two years opposite Glynis Johns. In the West End, she supported Jean Simmons – they also did the American tour – and in the 1976 screen version, Elizabeth Taylor, who became a close friend.

'Stephen became my honorary nephew, and my devotion to him led me to play sixty cities and cover some 30,000 miles in *Side By Side*. Alas, Kansas City was my downfall. Literally – over an iron pole at the railway station at 2.30 in the morning with few if any lights on. Shattered my knee, dislocated my right arm ... Still not my old self, but what the hell. Life does go on, with or without its little jolts, doesn't it?'

4

Joan Greenwood

*During a good ten minutes of our interview at London's
Strand Palace Hotel – over sherry trifles – Joan
Greenwood interrogated me about my recent trip to Italy.
'Ah, the Italian scene,' she intoned in that famous plummy
voice. 'I do have a Continental soul …' Though she always
kept Hollywood at arm's length, the once-beautiful blonde
with hazel-green eyes had been a leading cinema attraction
in Britain and Europe. At the end of our session she huskily
pleaded, 'Do emphasize that in spite of my film
opportunities I didn't give up the stage. I did not choose the
easier way.'*

'**M**y childhood was divine, or so I thought at the
time,' remembered Joan Greenwood
(1921-87). 'It seems boring in retrospect, at
least in the telling. I was even born in Chelsea, surely not
London's most exciting locality! Personally, in reading
biographies I always find the childhoods the one section one
can skim right through. They're terribly important in
shaping our lives, but make uniformly dull reading.

'I was no more outstanding as a child than the next one,

though I did have a very low voice for a girl. One acquaintance of ours advised me, after I'd evinced a passion for acting, that my voice would have to be offset by "beauty, grace and femininity". Well, during the 1940s, the Americans described me as a British Lauren Bacall. I was not unflattered, although I did wonder why she wasn't the American Joan Greenwood.'

There was more than surface similarity between the beguiling young actresses, despite Bacall's tougher personality and more direct screen characters. Both actresses were Jewish, but Betty Perske willingly changed her name. Joan Greenwood did not. 'I did not receive summonses from Hollywood. I was seen by studio chieftains as an alternative Vivien Leigh. However, it was unequivocally understood that I should change my names.

'I couldn't remain a Joan, because of Miss Crawford, and I couldn't remain a Greenwood, for the heads of the studios were trying desperately to create a standardized product. I refused to relinquish my name or identity. I decided to make good on talent, not on a depersonalized name.'

That Joan's father Earnshaw Greenwood was a famous painter was a factor in her family pride. Both parents fostered her interest in the arts, and at eight she commenced dancing lessons. Her goal was to become a ballerina. 'I have experienced an undying and gratifying love for the ballet ... Perhaps the role I most missed not having, for I was a bit too old, was dear Claire Bloom's ballerina in Charlie Chaplin's exquisite *Limelight* [1952].' Sadly, Joan's weak heart forced her to change tracks, and at seventeen she joined RADA (Royal Academy of Dramatic Art).

'I was an only child, therefore utterly and blissfully spoiled by my family. For so much of my life, I took great pleasure in being the youngest one in my circle.'

In 1938 the petite (5' 1") actress made her stage début as Louisa in Molière's *The Robust Invalid*. The following year, she appeared in *Little Ladyship* and played Little Mary in *The Women*. In 1940 she was seen in her first motion picture,

John Smith Wakes Up. She continued playing small parts until what she termed her 'official discovery' by actor-director Leslie Howard (born Leslie Howard Stainer).

'Mr Howard put me into *The Gentle Sex* [1943, which he co-helmed]. It's not well known ... Tragically, it was the last film before his death' – in a war-time airplane crash, flying between Portugal and England. Reportedly, Joan's despondency over his passing then kept her from the screen until 1945.

She told me, 'In no sense did I become a star overnight, either on stage or in pictures. On the stage, the first thing everyone noticed was my voice.' It would be described as 'a libido contralto' and 'gargling with champagne'. (Barbra Streisand imitated it for her role as an English aristocrat in *On a Clear Day You Can See Forever*.) 'What made my voice outstanding to audiences was that it issued forth from such a small body. Had I been taller, it would not have been so notable.'

Yet being short had its advantages. In 1941 Joan played Wendy in *Peter Pan*, and toured in the part in 1942. 'Once I was in a movie, I didn't appear so diminutive, and my voice was put into perspective. Then it became my face which was noticed, and during that period, if an actress had pleasing looks, many critics held that she had little or no talent.

'My appearance was an asset on the screen, but a bit detrimental on stage ...'

In 1943 Joan succeeded another budding British star, Deborah Kerr, in Bernard Shaw's *Heartbreak House*, then spent the rest of the year touring for ENSA (Entertainments National Service Association) – 'a small part of the war effort, but the patriotic thing to do, and a jolly opportunity to perfect one's craft before large audiences.' In 1944, in Britain, she toured as Ophelia in *Hamlet* and Celia in Ben Jonson's *Volpone*. 'Any tour was a splendid education!'

In 1945 she toured further in a variety of roles, among them Lady Teazle, Cleopatra and Nora (in *A Doll's House*). 'As I matured a little, my looks became more of an asset, since I was no longer so girlish.'

Also in 1945, she returned to the screen, contracting first with the Rank Organisation and later Ealing, where she made the comedies with which she is now most closely associated. Through the mid 1940s, she kept busy in mostly forgettable films such as *The Man Within* (US title *The Smugglers*), *The October Man* and *The White Unicorn* (US: *Bad Sister*). 'Perhaps my earliest films are best consigned to the recesses of memory.

'None were shamefully poor, but I'm afraid I couldn't be much help if you wanted specific facts or dates. It all now seems a lovely muddle.'

The 1948 *Saraband For Dead Lovers* (*Saraband* in the US, where *Dead* was considered a fatal title word) brought Joan Greenwood to the cinematic fore. 'It was hopelessly romantic and tragic,' she recalled. 'I was the wife who was cast aside, hopelessly in love with Stewart Granger but badly treated by fate and a fat, ugly and ambitious husband.

'In Britain this movie is still fresh. It's a true and timeless love story. If it's old-fashioned or at all out of favour now, it might be because of the ending, in which the wife is all but imprisoned, left to wither away and be forgotten. Yet it did happen, so one can't blame the film-makers.'

Critic Billie Flint felt, 'Miss Greenwood is magnificently plush, understatedly sexy and heartbreakingly ill-fated as the wife the future George I left behind in Germany ... The period outfits are sumptuous and the performances ripe, above all Greenwood and [Flora] Robson as contrasting specimens of herstory, the former young and aching to love, the latter old, corrupt and fecklessly substituting lust for love.'

The same year, Joan was ideally cast as Lady Caroline Lamb in *The Bad Lord Byron*. She explained, 'I adored historical pictures. Not only the marvellous costumes and hairdos and the drama of royal spectacle, but the sense that as non-fiction they could be more significant ...'

Nineteen-forty-nine brought an enduring comedy gem, *Whisky Galore,*from Compton Mackenzie's novel based on a true story about a ship wrecked off a Scottish island in the Outer Hebrides in 1941. (The title was changed for the American market to *Tight Little Island*, as *Whisky* was taboo.) In the ship's hold were some 50,000 cases of Scotch headed for the USA but coveted by locals deprived by war-time shortages of their cherished 'water of life'. Under cover of night, the islanders 'rescue' as many cases as they can.

'We had a marvellous time during the shooting,' reminisced Greenwood. 'It was shot on the Isle of Barra, called Todday in the film. Naturally, it was a charming and somewhat daring comedy, but on another level it was about the Scots outsmarting the English, and yet everybody in Britain loved it, and it became an international hit. I continue to receive effusive compliments on behalf of the entire delightful cast.'

Joan played an ordinary young woman for a change, and found that 'It was more of a demanding assignment for me to make the character engaging to an audience. For example, in *Saraband* I was a princess trying to escape with a count – that would naturally hold an audience's attention!'

The star's luck continued shining in 1949 with the classic jewel *Kind Hearts and Coronets*, which made famous the versatile Alec Guinness as a flock of stuffy aristocrats. Joan shared leading lady honours with Valerie Hobson, best remembered as the Baroness Frankenstein and the real-life wife of the main participant in the early 1960s Profumo Affair which toppled Britain's Conservative government.

'I played Sibella, which in Italian means 'so beautiful'. It was one of my most fabulous parts. She was a young lady who flirts and purrs but in the end chooses wealth and position over true love.' As such, she shuns leading man Dennis Price, but in time vies with Hobson for his affections after he manages to kill off the eight D'Ascoynes who stood between him and a dukedom. Said one critic, 'Joan's Sibella tempts and taunts in a voice that smoothly combines treacle and cyanide.'

'Originally,' stated Greenwood, 'Sir Alec was offered four of the [family] roles. He himself proposed playing them all. His acting feat was no small part of the film's great popularity, and I am told it was liked even better by the Americans.' Guinness was named 1950's Best Actor by America's National Board of Review, and the film one of the year's Ten Best.

But American censorship intervened, requiring Sibella — by then a married woman — to keep her hat on while visiting Price at his residence. 'The American censor believed that if I'd removed my hat in a man's room, we would have been depicting immorality and tempting impressionable youth!'

In 1951 Joan starred in *Young Wives' Tale*, now chiefly noted for a young Audrey Hepburn's small role: 'I thought Miss Hepburn was enchanting, and that it was only a matter of time until she too would find her niche. She had, and has, a splendid voice,' whose mellifluousness was early on compared to Greenwood's. That same year yielded another screen hit, *The Man in the White Suit*, starring Alec Guinness. The innovative comedy concerns a practically indestructible fabric, developed by chemist Alec, which causes more problems than it solves.

'I was off my cinematic pedestal once more, playing the mill owner's daughter who loves the sweet, unassuming man who cannot see that his invention threatens an entire industry ... When you think about it, didn't I have the most splendid run of luck, appearing in all those warmly esteemed pictures, the like of which we shall never see again?'

Later in 1951, Joan went to France to co-star with French heart-throb Gérard Philipe in *Monsieur Ripois* (*Mr Peek-a-Boo* in Britain). 'He was a stunningly handsome and highly sensitive personality, and I received innumerable letters from Continental cinema-goers who waxed poetic about how romantic a pair we were. By another token, one London critic sniffed that we were "too delicate" to be universal film heroes. That was the era when needless realism was starting to pervade films, and the purported heroes were becoming more violent.'

In 1952 she essayed one of her most famous characterizations, Gwendolyn Fairfax in Oscar Wilde's *The Importance of Being Earnest*. Sir Anthony Asquith helmed the perfected screen version which boasted Edith Evans as Gwendolyn's gorgon mother Lady Bracknell, Michael Redgrave as Earnest and Margaret Rutherford as Miss Prism. 'A sheer and utter delight,' cooed Joan. 'I was privileged to be among that company, and was not alone in the realization that we were immortalizing both the play (for the first time!) and the legendary performances of Dames Edith and Margaret.'

The Greenwood beauty, voice and elegance captured and defined Miss Fairfax as an upper-crust dream vision vacillating between acquiring her ideal man (his 'name produces [musical] vibrations ...') and observing her mother's absurdly Victorian proprieties ('Come, dear, we have already missed five if not six trains. To miss any more might expose us to comment on the platform.') Working with Edith Evans was 'easier than one might imagine from viewing that film. It is my firm opinion that she alone could have played Lady Bracknell. Yet as an individual she was very dear, a kind and generous person. As an utterly professional actress, she would never have allowed her ego or reputation to influence the other players' feelings or interpretations.

'When *Earnest* comes on the telly now, I can watch it over and over again. I still get letters addressed to Miss Fairfax ... But I was so young and lovely then, and she such a calculating little shrew-in-training – clearly following in her mother's footsteps! – that I must view her – the character and even the actress – as another person entirely.'

Meanwhile, back on the stage, Joan resumed her theatrical career in 1948, and in 1951 played Peter Pan. 'I saw Peter as a great challenge to my femininity, and hope I was fairly convincing! He's great fun to play, and when one critic described me as 'elfin' in the role, I was charmed and delighted!'

In 1954 she made her Broadway début in T.S. Eliot's poorly received *The Confidential Clerk*. 'I was bowled over by New York City, its immensity, height and frantic energy. The theatre community was most welcoming – theatre, you know, is theatre wherever one goes …'

The same year, she reteamed with Gérard Philipe and Valerie Hobson in *Knave of Hearts* (*Lovers, Happy Lovers* in the US). It was Hobson's last film; she retired at thirty-seven. Joan opined, 'What a will of iron it must take! I could never retire and then stick to it … It went to my heart that we lost her to pictures, but there is such an astounding range of personalities among actors, and each has his own method of happiness. I was always jolly well relieved that when I did a play which didn't please many people, I could move to the screen.'

Joan's second 1954 movie was *Father Brown*, starring Alec Guinness and retitled *The Detective* in America. 'We were old chums, always happy to work together. No "movie star" pretensions about dear Alec, or any other kind! And if his talent dominated the film, that was all right, for a solid hit always proved a tonic to my spirits. It's so dispiriting, but one works just as hard on a project which draws little enthusiasm from the public as one does on a project which seizes their fancy.

'All too often, it's the unpopular episodes one remembers. Even if one doesn't discuss them for print.'

In 1955 Joan succeeded Lilli Palmer as the love-prone witch Gillian in *Bell, Book and Candle*. She also went to California to do her first Hollywood movie. 'As a newcomer, I was deluged with reporters who asked my every opinion about their city and country. Naturally I had to be tactful as well as honest. I said I was astonished that no one else went walking in Beverly Hills, that when I did so, people would stop their cars to inquire if mine had broken down and I needed a ride.

'I was enchanted by the wonderful California fruit, although the lettuce was decidedly inferior, and when I ordered a salad, it came drenched in an abominable sauce called Thousand Islands. I still don't know which islands those are! The Hollywood press had a field-day with my remarks about the local tea. It's the water, you see – nobody's fault, but American tea is nowhere as good, so I drank only coffee.

'What made the tea even worse was the teabags. One couldn't help but taste the cloth!'

The Hollywood film was *Moonfleet*, directed by Fritz Lang – 'one of those angry, cartoonish German directors' – and co-starring Stewart Granger, George Sanders and Viveca Lindfors. The swashbuckling historical melodrama, 'in Cinemascope, no less', was set on the stormy Cornish coast, but shot in Oceanside, California. Film historian John Kobal called it 'a gothic story with all the trappings – a churchyard, wind, owls hooting at night, thunderstorms, mystery houses, and a rich, almost Dickensian atmosphere, superb music, costumes, and superior art direction and rich photography to enthral the viewer.'

Not a financial success, *Moonfleet*'s reputation grew over the years, and Lang, who had disowned it after MGM added a happy ending, later reclaimed it. Greenwood, whose last film it was until 1958, revealed, 'I was made glaringly aware of my function as ornamentation. To MGM, the most important aspect of my performance was my hair colour. They dyed it dozens of shades – blonde, orange, carrot, topaz, names I'd never heard of. It's a wonder I had any hair left on my head!

'In the final analysis, it's a very special film, and I did appear quite beautiful, like a fairy-tale character. Mr [Miklos] Rozsa's music added yet another dimension of other-worldliness, and I must say, the colours on the screen were vivid and luscious, almost edible!'

Back in Britain, Joan continued on stage in name parts like *Lysistrata* and *Hedda Gabler*, as well as in more contemporary plays which often failed to find large audiences. Cecil Beaton hit the nail on the head: 'Miss Greenwood is ideally suited to costume dramas and comedies, but nowadays period pieces are a dying breed.' Beaton's Regency designs for Streisand's costumes and coiffures in *On A Clear Day* were admittedly inspired by Joan's in *Saraband For Dead Lovers* and *Moonfleet*.

In 1958, at thirty-seven, the British actress did one more Hollywood movie, *Stage Struck*, playing the older woman in the remake of *Morning Glory*, a 1930s Katharine Hepburn vehicle. The role of the dewy, ambitious young actress went to Susan Strasberg, daughter of method coach Lee Strasberg. Henry Fonda was top-billed, and the film was a flop.

'It was not an emotionally positive experience. Mr Fonda was frostily proper ... and it signified my professional transition to second female lead – as a screen actress – which, particularly with Hollywood, is quite a depressing change ... My character was rather frost-bitten, and in spite of a top-drawer cast, nobody went [to movie-houses]. One of the critics said it was an emotionally distancing story because Mr Fonda was too old for Miss Strasberg. A valid point, for although it went unsaid, he was a bit too old for me too.'

Greenwood's next film would be the sci-fi adventure *Mysterious Island* (1962), and her remaining screen roles were all in the supporting category.

But if her career was slowing down in the 1960s, her personal life took on new prominence. In 1960 she wed for the first time, marrying actor André Morell (né André Mesritz) in Jamaica. The British actor played a small army of authority figures in films like *Stage Fright, Bridge On the River Kwai, Ben Hur, Judith, She* and *Pope Joan*. Greenwood, who rarely alluded to her private life, explained:

'André and I became friends first. That is the basis of any lasting relationship. We had much in common, and he was a kind man, a fine actor and a wonderful companion.' In 1960, she became pregnant with their only child, a son. She remained married to Morell until his death in 1978.

In April, 1961, Joan returned to the stage in *The Irregular Verb to Love*. Next year, she did *Uncle Vanya*, and reprised *Hedda Gabler* a few years later. 'As a mother, I eased away a bit from the stage's demanding schedule.' In 1963 she had a small but impactful role in Tony Richardson's international film smash *Tom Jones*. She was in her costumed glory again as the loftily lusty Lady Bellaston, who insinuatingly informs handsome Lotharios, 'My doors are always open to people of fashion ...'

Edith Evans was asked about her co-star's performance: 'Joan Greenwood can elevate any trollop to nobility, while her sophisticated voice can fuel the male imagination no matter how apparently innocent her role.'

Despite *Tom Jones*' box-office power, Joan had a minor, indifferent role in Disney's *The Moon-Spinners* (1964), a Hayley Mills vehicle which featured André Morell and brought silent screen star Pola Negri out of retirement. 'The script's level and its villains were rather juvenile, influenced by the James Bond fantasies prevalent at the time, but aimed at the very young fans who idolized Hayley Mills.

'It was lovely working with André, although I wish it could have been more in tandem, and more often ... Miss Negri was frankly fantastic. She recounted the most outlandish tales about herself – her halcyon days, and purported lovers and conquests ... Then she would retell them with details as well as important facts completely altered! She acted as if she'd never stopped being a big movie star. It didn't become her ...'

After *The Moon-Spinners*, Joan ignored the screen, and vice-versa, until the 1970s. In the late 1960s she stressed better-known stage plays, i.e., *Fallen Angels*, *Candida* and *The Chalk Garden*. Unlike many stage stalwarts, she did not miss the lack of Shakespeare in her repertoire. 'I've a jolly patriotic respect for the Bard, but I know that others can better interpret him. I am the first to applaud them. Audiences like to see me in rather more contemporary fare, although nothing *too* drastic.'

Basil Dearden, her director in *Saraband For Dead Lovers*, offered, 'Joan is one of the closest things we have to a Hollywood star. Her presence can fill up the screen, but her technical abilities [on stage] are more limited than some actresses', though she's a fine crowd-pleaser ... What happened with Joan is that she became a happy and contented wife-mother, and her happy home life has dulled the edge of her ambition.'

The occasional actress allowed, 'When you're young and see you still have a big chance, you try to move towards it. I did, yet I was never a great fighter, willing to create enemies and live in turmoil in order to obtain whatever I wanted. Looking back, I don't think I was wrong to have been less grasping than certain actresses of my physical type, nor to have waited so long before settling down.

'For, once I found my bliss, it lasted me.'

In 1973 she co-starred in Terence Rattigan's *In Praise of Love*. The playwright told *Films and Filming*, 'Miss Greenwood is glad to be treading the boards again ... She insists upon remarkably few of a star's prerogatives, and ignores past triumphs and dwells solely in the here and now.'

In 1977 she made her first films since 1971. Both *The Uncanny* and *The Hound of the Baskervilles* cast her in a less attractive, even harsh light. She recalled, 'The *Hound* remake was by and large quite amusing. It starred Peter Cook and Dudley Moore, also Kenneth Williams ... I came across as a dreadful old harridan with the longest tongue you ever saw! I'm afraid the special effects were quite exaggerated.'

In 1978 she made her final movie, *The Water Babies*, with James Mason. Both stars' screen images had shifted dramatically with time, from young, appealing and centre-stage to prematurely aged, villainous and/or grotesque, and frequently miscast as well as under-used. 'The worst thing about film producers,' Mason once commented, 'is their short memories.'

After Morell's passing in 1978, Joan did less stagework, preferring the greater freedom afforded by TV parts. In 1979 she appeared in the telefilm *The Flame Is Love*, noting, 'They think of me if they require an older actress who suggests wealth and breeding.' Her time off the small screen was taken up by her son Jason, her friends, and favoured activities such as reading, sleeping and 'attending circuses – as a child, I used to think the lady in pink was literally a God-send!'

In 1982, Greenwood filled in for the late Celia Johnson in the play *The Understanding* with Ralph Richardson. He found, 'She has a droll but devastating sense of humour. She ought to be doing yards and yards of comedy, but I understand she's quite the homebody now.' There were rumours of illness, as her looks faded fast, and instead of gaining weight she grew thinner. Away from the limelight, she did not have to cope with reporters' questions, but by the mid-1980s chose to revive her TV career with sitcoms like *Girls On Top*, mini-series like *Ellis Island* and genteel dramas like the BBC's Miss Marple series.

Joan's frail and aged appearance opposite a much older but more vital Joan Hickson as Jane Marple shocked many viewers. Upon completing her tea-guzzling scenes in Agatha Christie's *At Bertram's Hotel*, Greenwood informed the press, 'I feel wonderful, and do not foresee any need to retire from television. The pace is brisk, but the conditions and brevity are most agreeable.' Rediscovered by producers, albeit for token roles, she kept on working until two weeks before her fatal heart attack.

'You mightn't guess it,' she beamed after a first-rate sherry trifle, 'but in the movies I used to be a *femme fatale*. My eyes and voice were the main cause of that … But roles like that put one under a terrible strain, because if a given film failed, the leading lady's persona and desirability were called into question, and one couldn't but feel rather inadequate.

'Now that I flit from one role to the next, I'm having a more carefree time of it. I don't even need worry myself with the outcome; I watch it on the telly, and it's all a lovely surprise, and I know that eventually the telephone will ring with another divine little offer ...'

After Joan Greenwood died at sixty-five, film critic Tony Verdugo wrote, 'She will always be Gwendolyn, Sibella, Lady Caroline and a bevy of other beautiful ladies of quality and cunning who continue to enrich our movie-watching habit.'

5

Dame Celia Johnson

Celia Johnson once said, 'I often did things later in life than most of my contemporaries.' Thus, she didn't receive the DBE until her penultimate year, 1981, and did not move from stage star to film star until well into her thirties, nor start a family until her thirties. Although she worked in theatre most of her life, she is best remembered for her classic, ineffably British films. It was my first viewing of Brief Encounter *which prompted me to interview Celia Johnson in 1978, in an Italian restaurant in London. Owing to 'family matters', she had to leave early – which was in keeping with her reputation as an actress who put her family first.*

Probably the most famous British film of the 1940s was *Brief Encounter* (1945), via Noël Coward and starring Celia Johnson and Trevor Howard. It was director David Lean's third film, his third from a Coward story – all three starred Celia Johnson. But at the time, the eventually oft-imitated and parodied classic did not promise to become a popular or a critical hit. Lean much later recalled:

'I still have an affection for *Brief Encounter*. I have never really got over it. We were making *Great Expectations* when it came out and I had the first print during our location work on the Romney Marshes. We got it down to the local cinema and screened it as a sneak preview. It started, and during the first love scene a woman in the front row started laughing, a terrible cackling chicken's laugh.

'Then everyone else in the cinema started to laugh. And every love scene that came up, this woman started to laugh and the whole cinema was rolling in the aisles. I went back in the evening wondering how I could get into Denham Laboratories and burn the negative. I was so terribly ashamed of my work.

'So every time anyone mentions *Brief Encounter* I think, "Oh, yes, very nice in the art houses, but what the hell happened out of town?" A lesson in humility may be food for everyone – but I didn't need a lesson in humility in those days. I was a very frightened young man.'

Noël Coward felt that the central performances were crucial to the film's success. He allowed, 'Neither actor was overly attractive. They did not distract, and nor did they lift it into the realm of the gossamer or ethereal. They were splendid actors playing very real people.' As for the romance, he theorized, 'Rachmaninoff's Second Piano Concerto was – excuse the pun – instrumental. He supplied the heightened lushness, the theatricality that elevated an ordinary romance into something quite, quite indelible. We should almost have given him co-writing credit.'

(Interestingly, the majority of Coward's nine playlets produced collectively in 1936 as *To-Night at 8.30* have been filmed, including *Brief Encounter* from *Still Life*.)

Celia Johnson took on the unforgettable role of Laura while taking five years off from the stage to rear a family. Coward, her admirer and star-maker, noted, 'I once said that Celia Johnson could become one of the world's greatest actresses if she didn't keep having babies all the time. This was received with such gales of laughter and was quoted in the press, and I am unable to see anything funny in it at all. It is a statement of my sincere belief that Celia's domesticity is more important to her than is her theatrical vocation.'

Though *Brief Encounter* was not initially a financial success, the critics were ecstatic. London reviewers called it one of the best films to come out of Britain. Hollywood nominated Johnson for the Academy Award; she won the New York Film Critics' Best Actress award for 1946. America's National Board of Review listed *Brief Encounter* among the year's ten best films.

In 1978, the pre-Dame Celia mused, 'I was famous, or infamous, at least in entertainment circles, for my five-year plans. Not unlike the Soviets! But they weren't really plans, or even unalterable. It simply turned out that there were about five years between *Brief Encounter* and my next picture.'

David Lean explained, 'Her American fans could not "figure out" her motives! She was a film star, one of Britain's biggest film stars, an accomplished one, yet she didn't necessarily follow up her triumphs, and she didn't seek out the best-paid opportunities or fling herself in Hollywood's direction ... In short, she was a contented actress and lady.'

Trevor Howard, Alec to her Laura, remembered, 'She didn't seem to spend any time wondering where her next assignment was coming from. Without wishing to sound at all flippant or disrespectful, I may say that at times she gave the impression of a happy homemaker who was taking time off to work in a motion picture – with a stunning result, for she *was* Laura. One had the feeling that if she, Celia, were in the same position that Laura found herself in, she would react and behave accordingly.'

Johnson reminisced that she 'felt somewhat toward Trevor as my character did – mildly infatuated, which she was in the beginning, however much she may have denied it to herself. In my case, I consciously admitted to myself that Trevor was a good-looking and very appealing man and gentleman, and for me it was naturally no more than that. From then on, the actress took over, and we were buoyed up and floated along by Sir Noël's beautiful words of romantic longing and restraint.'

Coward was adamant that a key to *Brief Encounter*'s timeless and universal appeal and artistic integrity was the non-consummation of Alec and Laura's romance. 'There have been countless cheap and utterly banal pictures about a man and woman, married or otherwise, going at it in a backroom or back street. The fact that Laura and Alec held out, and held on to their principles, provides the temporary frustration and the permanent satisfaction with which audiences view *Brief Encounter*, then and now.

'Of course, the pair's marital fidelity was dictated by the censorship of that period. But I'm convinced it was all to the good of the story and its emotional impact.' Sir Noël did not believe any of the remakes worked nearly as well, including the highly publicized 1975 British telefilm starring Sophia Loren and Richard Burton. The playwright-director quipped that Loren, though a fine actress, had a face made for seduction, while Celia Johnson's was 'a face made for suffering'.

When I asked Ms Johnson what she thought of the Loren-Burton remake, she tactfully confessed, 'The story holds up. The characters are beyond nationality or era,' proved by Loren's Italianized characterization, 'even though they've been criticized in some quarters as "too English". But I did hear there were grumblings from those who prefer the original and saw no need to change it. But the actors did do a fine job ...'

She added that the change from black-and-white to colour was not 'exactly jarring, but it brought the whole thing on to a more realistic level. In my opinion, what black-and-white provided was a dream-like feeling; I think it left more room for the viewer's imagination and suspension of belief ... And Eileen Joyce's rendition of the Second Piano Concerto was superb in our version, and missed in the newer one.

'It really is practically impossible to compete with memories and nostalgia, and that overlay of status which gets placed on to a classic. Besides, I don't think one could compete with such original talents as Noël Coward and David Lean ... or

Rachmaninoff, for that matter.'

Celia Johnson was born in Richmond, Surrey, on 18 December 1908, the daughter of a member of the Royal College of Surgeons. After a good education in England and on the Continent, she studied at RADA, then made her stage bow in 1928 at Huddersfield's Theatre Royal, playing Sarah in Shaw's *Major Barbara*. The next year, she made her London début at the Lyric, Hammersmith, taking over from Angela Baddeley as Currita in *A Hundred Years Old*. She then began touring, and in London played opposite stars like Gerald du Maurier and Gladys Cooper.

The actress's career was not focused on Shakespeare or the classics, and her progress was steady but slow. She was pretty rather than beautiful, and one critic called her 'plaintive-looking'. Her hair's distinctive wave was copied by many, but 'I had no realistic hopes of being a glamour girl'. Instead, she was habitually cast as the girl-next-door, until she made the transition to the woman-next-door – the ideal housewife.

In 1931 she succeeded Madeleine Carroll in *After All* at the Criterion. Johnson said, 'I was fascinated by her blonde, doll-like beauty. So like a porcelain figure, she was ... She'd been acting in films for a few years already, and she asked whether I had any ambitions regarding film. I may have had, but I didn't retain high hopes, and managed to ask her no more than a few questions about film acting.'

Later in 1931, Johnson made her New York début as Ophelia to Raymond Massey's glowering Hamlet. John Mason Brown wrote of her 'touching pathos when [the] mad scenes are reached'. In London, play followed play, but she did not experience her first long run until 1933, in *The Wind and the Rain*, which ran two years. 'It was something of a relief to be in a play that people obviously liked and kept coming back to.

'There were a few times when I privately questioned whether I should continue making a career of the theatre, or instead settle down and do the expected thing. In those days, it wasn't automatically assumed that a girl could do both ... I sometimes thought I was prolonging my girlhood by playing those roles and enjoying my existence, rather than either marrying or playing the classics as a truly serious actress would. However, they didn't usually put me into the classics ...'

In 1934 Celia made her first movie, *Dirty Work*. She failed to set the screen world on fire, and only returned in 1941, in two shorts. In 1942, her screen career was taken in hand by Noël Coward, and the rest, as they say, is history. 'For the most part, I liked what I was doing [on the stage]. After doing the one picture, I said to myself, "Well, now I've done that," and that was that ... In the 1930s, motion picture stars were unbelievably beautiful and excruciatingly glamorous.

'Since I did not remotely resemble Madeleine Carroll or Marlene Dietrich, I went back to the stage as a matter of course ... I truly didn't feel that film acting was all that fulfilling. The fragmentation of scenes was alien to me, and the lack of a chance to improve on a performance each night, as in the theatre, was disappointing.'

In 1935, Celia Johnson wed writer-explorer Peter Fleming, who had a big country estate near Henley-on-Thames. Queried about her marriage and family life in 1978, the actress responded, 'Wonderful. I married for love, and not out of others' expectations. I made my own choices, and they paid off handsomely.' She continued acting on the stage.

In 1936 she was Elizabeth Bennet in *Pride and Prejudice*, in 1940 she starred in Daphne du Maurier's *Rebecca*, and in 1942 followed Vivien Leigh at the Haymarket as Jennifer in *The Doctor's Dilemma*. She then took five years' leave from the theatre to commence a family.

'It was time – time for me to have a family if ever I was going to do so ... They were lovely years. I had the best of both worlds with my home life and those extraordinary films

Noël Coward created. His support was more than flattering, it was a great confidence-booster. Because the war was on, we all gave of our best, and I think the quality of the films concerned was a reflection of everybody doing their utmost and putting self second to the country and our war effort.'

In 1942, ironically the year she chose to vacate the stage, Celia Johnson was picked to co-star in the war classic *In Which We Serve*. Its producer-director and star was Noël Coward, who also wrote the story. To share directorial duties, the busy star hired David Lean, then Britain's top film editor. It was an auspicious start to Lean's distinguished directorial career. The movie featured a number of newcomers, among them actors Michael Wilding and Richard Attenborough. It co-starred John Mills, Bernard Miles, Kay Walsh and Joyce Carey.

In Which We Serve tells of a British destroyer, HMS *Torrin*, and the men who serve aboard the ship at the launch of the Second World War. It was done in semi-documentary fashion and made ample use of flashbacks. Self-avowedly propagandistic, the film aimed at patriotic morale-building, and was popular at home and abroad. The New York Film Critics named it the Best Picture of the year, and Hollywood awarded a Special Oscar to Noël Coward. The National Board cited it as the year's best, and Coward fondly deemed it 'an emotional highpoint of my creative life'.

Two years later, Coward, Lean, Celia Johnson and John Mills reteamed for *This Happy Breed*. It was Lean's first solo directorial effort. Due to *In Which We Serve*'s success, it was made in colour. It was also the first movie from Cineguild, a production company formed by Lean, producer Anthony Havelock-Allan and cameraman Ronald Neame. The story of two decades in the lives of the working-class Gibbons family, *This Happy Breed* spans the inter-war years 1919 to 1939. Somewhat more naturalistic than *In Which We Serve*, the film's ending is a muted one, partly because of the closing year.

Celia stated, 'It has been dismissed by some as a

soap-opera. In this day and age, that's hardly a compliment, but *This Happy Breed* was primarily a family saga – not completely dissimilar to the family sagas which have had such an impact on night-time television ... The acting was praised; we were described as displaying commendable restraint in depicting the joys and sorrows of an ordinary family.' What she neglected to say was that when *This Happy Breed* reached the USA three years later, the National Board of Review named Johnson the Best Actress of 1947.

By comparison, *Brief Encounter* reached the States in 1946, one year after its UK release. That, of course, was the tale of Laura and Alec, each married to another. Their new and innocent friendship becomes a romance which blossoms into a deeply felt love even while evading carnality. Because of their love for and commitment to their respective families, the two almost-lovers reluctantly and dramatically part company.

Ronald Neame, later himself a distinguished director, opined, 'Celia brought a nobility to the part. You could not expect from her anything but decency, yet she wasn't anachronistic or saintly. She was just the sort of person everyone would want to have for a friend or neighbour ... The opening scene, repeated near the end, was brilliant – powerfully demonstrating how differently we observe the very same scene when we know all the circumstances behind it ... I think audiences everywhere could identify on several levels with these two characters. There isn't one false note in the entire film. It is quite a perfect film.'

Did Johnson believe she was stereotyped by her most famous role and that movie's enduring acclaim?

She smiled mischievously. 'It seemed to me that anyone connected with film-making wished me to go on playing Laura into eternity! Happily, no one was really able to duplicate Noël's wonderfully literate but simple script. There was only one *Brief Encounter*. It would have been most unlikely that its impact could have been reproduced.

'I was typecast, to some degree, as a good wife and

mother. The three Coward films did that. They did it because they were well-written and well-acted. People want to think that screen characterizations are little more than an actor being himself. This short-changes the actor, but it's easy enough to comprehend. People did take a shine to Laura, and wanted to see her again. As a spectator, I could understand wanting to see Laura again, but as an actress, I wanted to do other things – at least to do variations on the good wife and mother. Thank goodness they didn't have this mania for sequels at the time!

'I didn't ponder trying to turn around and play a villain. As an actress, I could have brought it off, but it might have been too extreme a change, and too abrupt, for audiences to accept. And why do it just to shock audiences? ... I really wasn't overly ambitious. I thought it lucky when an actress could play someone like Laura, then play a demented murderess. But it simply wasn't in the cards for me.

'May we have some more tea – sorry, *espresso?*'

Two years after *Brief Encounter*, Celia made her stage comeback with the Old Vic Company at the New Theatre as Shaw's 'Saint Joan'. Although her return had been eagerly awaited, especially in the light of her Coward-engineered screen stardom, her Joan did not yield unanimous hurrahs. The praise was 'balanced' by criticism that Johnson's Maid of Orléans wasn't sufficiently fiery or strong. T.C. Worsley declared, 'Miss Celia Johnson is a sincere and gifted player ... To Saint Joan, for all her sincerity, she is at no point suited, not in voice, presence or weight. This is no fault of hers, but her acting fails to redeem it.'

Frequent co-star and friend Ralph Richardson offered, 'Celia is best at delineating those marvellous, underrated personalities which we call "everyday". There is another type of performer best equipped for representing unusual, even incredible characters. Few of us can do both ...'

(Looking briefly back, Ms Johnson told me, 'Some say we learn more from our mistakes than our successes. I think I have learned from both. But publicly, I'd rather talk about the positive than the negative, as there's no possibility of correcting a wrong that is past and gone.')

Again, the star shuttled between child-bearing and child-rearing, and the stage. In 1950 she made her screen comeback in *The Astonished Heart*, from Noël Coward's play, with Coward in the role enacted on stage by Michael Redgrave. It was directed by Anthony Asquith, who averred, 'Her strength is her naturalism. Celia is a first-rate stage actress. She is a better film actress, because the camera enhances her natural likeability and makes of her a genuine British heroine.'

Her *Astonished Heart* co-star Margaret Leighton frankly commented, 'Celia could have done well in Hollywood, had she been more aggressive ... The camera loved her, and she was that wife-mother apotheosis which moguls like Louis B. Mayer jumped at for so long. But she did not pursue film actively enough, and honestly, she didn't have quite enough SA [sex appeal] for Hollywood. Even Greer Garson had some.'

Also in 1950, Johnson toured Italy with the Old Vic Company as Viola in *Twelfth Night*. Back in London in 1951, she played Olga in *The Three Sisters*. Nineteen-fifty-two was unique in her career, for she made two of her infrequent movies that year, *I Believe In You* and *The Holly and the Ivy* (not released in the US until 1954). The more memorable of the two, the latter co-starred Ralph Richardson, Margaret Leighton and Denholm Elliott. A yuletide comedy-drama, it was a screen adaptation of Wynyard Browne's West End hit play.

The Holly and the Ivy's warmth begins with its Norfolk country vicarage setting and centres on Richardson as a widower of the cloth whose family gathers by his side during the holidays. His three offspring are soldier son Mick (Elliott), journalist daughter Margaret (Leighton) and the dutiful Jenny (Johnson), who has stayed on to take care of him and is now unable to leave him to marry her engineer fiancé.

Celia Johnson said, 'It was a poignant story about communication, and the lack of it in too many well-meaning families. The reconciliation scene [between Richardson and Leighton) was lovely, and I think it all pointed up how some parents don't feel or react to their own children's needs, even while tending the needs of those outside their families.' As for playing yet another long-suffering character, she laughed, 'What is termed "suffering" today was called "duty" then.

'I think Jenny was torn, as many daughters are and of course were, between looking after a parent and making a new, independent life for herself.' At any rate, Margaret's decision to come home to her reconciled father leaves Jenny free to fly away from the nest. With a firm underline to her voice, the actress added, 'I never look upon the women I played as weak or pitiful. That may be the perspective today, but at that time, they were seen by most people to be women of strong convictions ... I don't think I've ever played a character without backbone.'

The role of a typical British housewife was next on her agenda, in the cult film classic *The Captain's Paradise* (1953). Of Alec Guinness's two simultaneous wives, Celia was predictably the 'nice' one and Yvonne de Carlo (née Peggy Middleton!) the 'naughty' one. 'You may not believe it, but I didn't yearn to play [de Carlo's] character ... I read interviews with actors who say that they act so they can get away from themselves as much and as far as possible; to me, it sounds like an alternative to psychotherapy – or like self-indulgence.

'I don't try to distance myself from my real self, unless a role calls for it. When I do work, I'm influenced by the calibre of the material and the artists involved. Perhaps I'm just too average to have got very far away from myself!'

Johnson's clipped tones and nobly sweet performances often obscured her flair for comedy, which she amply displayed at the Cambridge Theatre in 1955 in William Douglas-Home's *The Reluctant Débutante*. Frank Granville-Barker wrote, 'The comedy could have been placed in no more capable hands than those of Celia Johnson and Wilfrid Hyde White, whose timing and throwaway of lines are impeccable. The former's portrayal of harassed social ambition is thoroughly captivating.'

Comedy, felt the actress, 'becomes more important as we age. I know I had no specific desire to get involved in comedy when I was younger. The young pine for the classics and Shakespeare and serious things. As we grow older, perhaps we need comedy more and can better appreciate it ... and play it better.

'There is no way to survive as a performer without a sense of humour, and a lot of actors dream of having a long run in a comedy. It is hard work, but really most gratifying. The laughter is a genuine sign of audiences' approval and gratification. Applause is very nice, needless to say, but it does fall under the category of good manners.'

When I inquired about the dictum that it is easy for an actor to make an audience cry, difficult to make them laugh, she became diplomatic: 'If I praise one of the two arts over the other, it will look as if I'm taking sides, and the arguments will never cease.' She smiled warmly. 'Besides, as in anything, it's not what one does, but how one does it.'

Her 1955 stage comedy was complemented by the touching 1955 movie *A Kid For Two Farthings*, helmed by Carol Reed and adapted by Wolf Mankowitz from his own story about life in London's East End. Reed had been attracted to the fairy-tale nature of the uplifting parable and to its folksy Jewish humour. He later remarked, 'Any success the picture has had is due in no small measure to Wolf's skilful, racy, warm and witty dialogue.'

In fact, it was the refined accents of Celia Johnson as the mother and Jonathan Ashmore as the boy which were blamed for detracting from the East End milieu. Johnson admitted, 'It was a wonderful family film, and I had a few reservations about the spoken dialogue – only. Even so, I was urged to do the picture, and have never regretted it.' The titular 'kid' is a little white goat which takes the fancy of a

Celia Johnson with Trevor Howard in *Brief Encounter*, 1945.
(*Aquarius Picture Library*)

Dame Celia with Maggie Smith in *The Prime of Miss Jean Brodie*,
1968. (*Doug McClelland*)

A 1920 portrait of Elsa Lanchester.

Lanchester as *The Bride of Frankenstein*, 1935.

Lanchester in *Northwest Outpost*, 1947.

six-year-old living with his mother in the shop of an old tailor who encourages him to think of it as a magical unicorn. The kid seemingly causes a string of 'miracles', then dies. The boy gets a new pet, and the return of his long-lost father is intimated.

A Kid For Two Farthings co-starred David Kossoff, Diana Dors and Brenda de Banzie. Reed did not overlook the criticism of the lead duo's accents, but emphasized 'Celia's motherly qualities and capacity for heroic endurance. Qualities like that overrode any discrepancy between her speech and that of the impoverished East Enders.'

Johnson did another movie in 1957, *The Good Companions*, then stayed away from the screen for eleven years.

In late 1957 at the Haymarket, the sometime movie star portrayed Isobel Cherry in Robert Bolt's *Flowering Cherry*, opposite Ralph Richardson. He claimed, 'I do not refer to anything in which we have appeared together, but it is my considered opinion that Celia Johnson is better than much of her stage material.' In 1960 she directed *Special Providence* at the St Martin's – 'a heady experience, one I should have taken up when I was younger' – then co-starred with Anthony Quayle in *Chin-Chin* as Pamela Puffy-Picq. Critic Peter Roberts wrote: 'Miss Johnson continues to get the utmost comedy out of the precise and orderly Englishwoman she is playing and at the same time makes the onlooker feel pity for the character's desperate unhappiness.'

A few years later, she acted in such light fare as *The Tulip Tree* and *Out of the Crocodile* before joining the National Theatre Company at the Old Vic in 1964 to play Mrs Solness in Ibsen's *The Master Builder*. She took over the role after Diana Wynyard died, sharing the spotlight with Maggie Smith and Michael Redgrave, who would lose his stage memory to Parkinson's disease. Celia's climactic confession scene about Mrs Solness's dolls eerily suggested madness, and won high praise via reviews and the kudos of her co-stars.

Redgrave stated, 'Her gentle aura is no less tranquil for the implication that there are emotions boiling beneath the surface, in much of her finest work.'

In 1965 she took over as Judith Bliss in Noël Coward's *Hay Fever*. The master enthused, 'The years merely refine Celia's technique, so smooth it seems effortless ... Her simplicity is an excuse for the shallow to underrate her talents.'

The following year found Celia playing Madame Ranyevskaya in *The Cherry Orchard*. As happened occasionally when she attempted a classic, she was trounced by certain reviewers. Peter Roberts of *Plays and Players* noted, 'Miss Johnson is a mannered actress who has thrived on her mannerisms in parts ranging widely ... But a new mannerism – a sort of pop-eyed stare – is developing, and it does not work as well as the others.

'At one moment this Mme Ranyevskaya looks perfectly normal. At another she takes on the appearance of a raving lunatic. It is extremely disconcerting.'

When I wondered how performers coped with the more personal of their notices, Johnson pursed her lips slightly and looked vaguely injured. 'That may be the very worst element of acting. A writer, say, is judged on his work and its merits. His looks and personality are not brought into the, uh, circle of fire. For some reason, it is easier to see one's work disparaged than to read personal, even impertinent, observations about one's physical self. It's most unsporting.

'But we must suffer the slings and arrows of the rare but hurtful individual – an apparently professional writer – who tries to be witty or clever at our expense.

'It hurts, and the best thing is to ignore the source, not to read it. Strangely, it finds its way to one's ears, and can affect a performance and an actor's morale ... There is no remedy for this genteel barbarism – some editors may even encourage it.

'We all have our preferences among particular actors or actresses, but I would never dream of judging an actress by her features or mannerisms.'

'Actresses,' I said, 'have it worse than actors. So often, Bette

Davis was reviewed more for her eyes or mannerisms than her performance, and Streisand is critiqued as much for her looks or aggressive personality as her singing or acting.'

'That's so, but what is particularly unfair is that we all have intrinsic little habits or mannerisms. But a given critic chooses, for whatever reason, to harp on the one theme. It has happened in abundance to Maggie Smith – she has no doubt the most famous wrists in the business!'

In 1968 Celia Johnson was back in films, this time in a supporting and distinctly non-sympathetic role. The film was *The Prime of Miss Jean Brodie*, directed by Ronald Neame; the role, that of the vindictive headmistress Miss McKay, who wants to rid the conservative Marcia Blaine School for Girls of the free-wheeling Miss Brodie (Maggie Smith). Johnson was Oscar-nominated, as was Smith, who copped the Best Actress Academy Award.

I asked Ms Johnson about this, a favourite movie of mine. We discussed the plot, characters and setting, then I inquired if she had liked Miss McKay? 'I understand her. She had a firm theory of education, but no tolerance for those with differing views. Miss Brodie didn't toe her line, so they were adversaries.'

Had she hesitated to play what amounted to the villain of the piece?

'Had Miss McKay been more black – less grey – I might have done. But it was a wonderful part in a wonderful film, so beautifully done by Ronald Neame and all concerned. We all received outstanding notices, and the film continues to generate what Miss Brodie might term new *aficionados*.'

I brought up a major discrepancy in the script. Though Brodie was supposedly liberal, she was represented as an outspoken fan of fascists Franco and Mussolini! Celia proposed, 'It may have been a plot device for discharging Miss Brodie from the school. Miss McKay had already failed, and it was only Miss Brodie's support for Franco, and the disloyalty of one student, that enabled Miss McKay to banish her from Marcia Blaine.

'You're right – it makes little sense, and may have been the writer's way of bringing Miss Brodie down a peg or two. Naturally, they stopped short of having her laud Hitler ... I did not win [the Oscar], but I was elated when Maggie won; she was an example of the rare instance when such an award goes to a deserving talent rather than a popular or local favourite.'

Alas, *Brodie*'s critical and commercial success did not result in many offers of screen work for Celia Johnson, and virtually none from Hollywood, where she was still deemed 'too British'. In the late 1970s and early 1980s she did further camera work in telefilms like *Les Misérables* and *The Hostage Tower*.

In the late 1960s, she reprised Judith Bliss in *Hay Fever* in Toronto, then travelled back to London with the production. At the Nottingham Playhouse in 1970, she was Gertrude to Alan Bates's Hamlet, moving to London with that production in 1971. She may have empathized with Bates, whose notices featured indignation that a movie icon should tackle the Bard, and in an allegedly less than worthy manner. Johnson then followed Peggy Ashcroft as Lady Boothroyd in *Lloyd George Knew My Father*.

'I have been teased for taking over others' characters in plays. What ought I to say? I didn't plan it, it happened ... I don't feel it's particularly disadvantageous, and I'm not ashamed to reveal the obvious – that the part probably wasn't offered to me in the first instance. But I do think it's better to have played a meaty role later than not at all.

'You find with age that false pride really isn't worth the accommodating.'

In 1974 and 1977, she enjoyed appearing in two Douglas-Home plays, *The Dame of Sark* and *The Kingfisher*. The second co-starred Ralph Richardson, of whom she said, 'He is a comforting and enlivening soul, on the stage and off. He tells me that I ought to work more often, and I ask him why? He never has an answer. But when we do work together, I again know what it is to work with a professional and unique talent.'

Did she miss doing more films?

'I would if they were good. I know it would be difficult to find roles or films as good as what I was privileged to do in the past. I don't dwell in the past, and am overall quite pleased with today, but I see little need to work for the sake of it. Particularly in a motion picture. A stage play may become an interesting 'failure' of which one is none the less proud. Too many films, box-office successes or not, are downright embarrassing ... The actors are more directly responsible for the relative success or failure of a play, and I like that responsibility.

'In a film today, most actors are just tiny pieces in what too often is a large and gruesome puzzle.'

Celia Johnson's cinematic heyday occurred when Britain's films were still thoroughly British. They had not been watered down and flattened out for the 'international' (Hollywood) market which in any case embraces only pictures selling violence, special effects and macho hype. Small wonder that she said, 'I feel more and more proud to have been in pictures like *In Which We Serve* and *Brief Encounter* with each passing year.'

The actress was created a Dame in 1981. Her final appearance was in 1982, starring opposite Ralph Richardson in Angela Huth's play *The Understanding*. After a few previews at the Strand Theatre, on 25 April 1982, Dame Celia had a stroke during a bridge game at her home in Nettlebed, then passed away.

6

Elsa Lanchester

Elsa Lanchester took to being interviewed like a duck to water. She never ran out of things to say, though as the interview wore on, she said them with diminishing enthusiasm. By the twilight of her life it was undeniable that she was known mainly for two roles: The Bride of Frankenstein *and as the wife of Charles Laughton. Lanchester relished what was left of her fame, but it rankled that usually she had to speak of Others, that hers was largely reflected fame.*

*T*he Bride of Frankenstein, directed in 1935 by the 'veddy' English James Whale, is widely considered the best horror film ever made. Did the woman who incarnated the title role agree with this assessment? 'I wouldn't dispute it,' she replied ambiguously. 'Whale had a flair for horror. He directed Charles's first American film, *The Old Dark House*, and he did *The Invisible Man* and of course *Frankenstein*. Also *Showboat* and other highbrow things, but now he's remembered for the macabre ones.'

Over the decades, specifically via television – Hallowe'en or any other night – *Bride* developed a cult following. Up to the last, Elsa would fill requests for autographed photos, as the cone-coiffed monster's mate. The eerie role became so identified with the offbeat performer that it stymied her career.

'I always knew,' she sighed, 'that Charles would be the bigger star. Which was as it should be. He had more talent, he was more ambitious and he worked harder at his craft. With me, it was more of a lark.

'But then we came to Hollywood and were temporarily seduced by the glamour. Believe me, glamour is the first illusion to go. But before it did, I thought – and Whale practically convinced me – that *Bride* could make me famous in my own right. Then I could write my own ticket, professionally.

'Well, *Bride* was Universal's first horror sequel, and obviously it wasn't their last! It did extremely well. But not for me ...' For one thing, Elsa was billed below Boris Karloff, Colin Clive (Baron Frankenstein) and even Valerie Hobson (the baroness). And, her impact notwithstanding, she had few scenes:

'They cut here and there, even more from the prologue, where I played Mary Shelley [author of *Frankenstein*] and looked the best I ever have on screen.' After a moment's reflection, she added, 'When it's shown on TV, they often cut the prologue altogether, to make room for the dog-food ads!'

(In 1985 the picture was weakly remade as *The Bride*, with Jennifer Beals as a flashdance-in-the-pan bride.)

Since there could be no other role quite like the *Bride*, Hollywood, where the Laughtons settled in the mid-30s, had trouble casting Elsa. Her pixie-ish humour and gamine quality eluded producers who frequently stuck her in Laughton movies or, as she grew less sylph-like, cast her as household help or quick-tempered nannies.

But, then, it was not an easy time for transplanted British actresses in general. 'Vamps and Continentals had a better chance,' Elsa pointed out. 'If I *had* to, I could slink about – and feel downright silly. I could do a passable German or Swedish accent, but not on a permanent basis.

'So, because I had an English accent and wasn't really pretty, Hollywood often cast me as a maid. That is to say,' she giggled, 'as a domestic ...'

Elizabeth Sullivan Lanchester was born in the London suburb of Lewisham, on 28 October 1902. 'For publicity's sake, Universal tried to change my birthday to 31 October. Until I screamed bloody murder!'

Edith Lanchester was an active suffragist and former teacher. She later became secretary to Eleanor Marx, Karl Marx's daughter, who translated *Madame Bovary* into English. James Sullivan, son of an Irish London policeman, worked in a black lead factory and was a militant trade unionist. Elsa's parents were committed socialists and icono-clasts; Edith Lanchester had chosen to cohabit with 'Shamus' Sullivan minus a marital contract. The result was kidnapping by her own father and brothers, and a brief but shocking enforced stay at a mental asylum.

The pair had two nonconformist children. Waldo, a future puppeteer, was five years older than Elsa, a natural bohemian who carried on in the family tradition. After 'training' with Isadora Duncan, she taught dance at thirteen, then ran a children's theatre, did 'snake dancing', posed for 'artistic' nude photos and was hired out as a co-respondent in divorce cases.

At sixteen she entered show business and for a time ran her own nightclub, the avant-garde Cave of Harmony. The canny entrepreneur subsequently revealed, 'We couldn't get a liquor licence, so we left the tops off cider bottles, and in a few weeks they'd become a little alcoholic.'

In 1927 the actress met Charles Laughton during West End rehearsals for *Mr Prohack*. The actor (born 1899) had already been referred to in print as a genius by James Agate. He found himself drawn to Elsa's kooky yet friendly nature, while she was attracted to his star stature and the fact that 'he was one of the few men who listened'. The two became fast friends, and within months decided to live platonically together.

In 1927 Elsa made her screen début in *One of the Best*, then appeared in *The Constant Nymph*. Next year, she and Laughton worked together in his first two films, the shorts *Bluebottles* and *Daydreams*. In spite of his ungainly looks, Laughton's overwhelming talent and presence made it clear that he had a cinematic future as a leading man. Therefore, and even though they had recently stopped living together, the homosexual star-to-be proposed marriage. Elsa accepted, and in 1929 they moved into Karl Marx's old house in Dean Street after a honeymoon trip to the Continent which also included Charles's mother and his brother Frank.

'You know how some people say "the honeymoon is over" after five or seven years? With Charles and me, the honeymoon was over on the honeymoon. Not just because of the relatives in attendance; his primary interests were his work and keeping up appearances. My primary interests, well, I hadn't yet discovered exactly what those were!'

The struggling actress continued shuttling between inconsequential films and the stage. 'We lived very modestly, but I socialized almost as much as I worked! I had so many friends in London, and I loved to go out, for London was a very lively – and safe – place then. I used to joke with Charles that if he ever did become a film star, he could make history by being the first actor to refuse to go to Hollywood!'

But he did, and he didn't. In 1932 Laughton was lured to Tinseltown, where in one year he starred in *The Old Dark House*, *If I Had a Million*, *Payment Deferred*, De Mille's *The Sign of the Cross*, *The Devil and the Deep* (a triangle with Gary Cooper and Tallulah Bankhead!) and *Island of Lost Souls*, from H.G. Wells's novel *The Island of Dr Moreau*.

Back in England the following year, Laughton recreated the title role in producer-director Alexander Korda's *The Private Life of Henry VIII*. The now legendary London Films production changed everything for Charles and Elsa, who played an amusing Anne of Cleves to her husband's lady-killing monarch. Ironically, it took a British picture to make Laughton a Hollywood superstar, with an Academy Award into the bargain.

About *Henry*, Elsa said, 'It was my best opportunity, to date. I knew I couldn't compete with the beautiful and very vain Merle Oberon [as Anne Boleyn], so my particular wife, who was German and known for her jollity, would have to impress the viewer with her humour ... Countless viewers over the years have told me they particularly liked Charles's and my scenes, that they were the comic highlight of the movie. Some critics remarked on the intimacy of our scenes, which I found funny, because after all, whatever our relationship was, Charles and I were also married ...'

She recalled, 'Charles was very much a celebrity in Hollywood [in 1932]. It delighted and unnerved him. But with *Henry*, he became so much the world figure, with such acclaim, that his confidence mushroomed overnight. He knew he would remain a star for a long time. As his confidence soared, so did mine. I immediately saw that via Charles I could get a steady stream of parts. What I didn't know was whether those parts would be worthwhile!'

In 1936 the duo acted again for Korda, in the costly flop *Rembrandt*. Elsa portrayed 'the third woman' in the painter's life, Hendrickje Stoffels, with whom he lived after she had been his servant and then gave birth to their child. The character did not show up until the film's second half. 'Korda gave me the smallest possible assignment. He had to give me something, because he went through me to get Charles to star for him again. But he disliked me and my acting.'

Asked why she thought *Rembrandt* did not have remotely the public appeal of *Henry*, Lanchester replied, 'It went over well in Holland. That was to be expected. I think they appreciated the authenticity of the movie – great pains and expenses were taken to get everything precisely *so*. The details were more authentic than in *Henry*, but perhaps in terms of sex and violence the painter was no match for the absolute monarch. I think somehow people expected *Rembrandt* to be even *more* of a spectacle, in that De Mille-like way. Whereas Rembrandt had really kind of a quiet, unspectacular life.

'I used to joke with Charles that we could have a sure-fire hit if somebody would shoot the life story of my parents. Charles would have played my father and I my mother, except that the parent I physically resembled was my father. Charles, of course, didn't resemble either.'

Meantime, 1935 had been a busy year for Elsa (and, though she didn't know it at the time, her high-point, profession-ally). She made her American film bow minus Charles in *David Copperfield*, directed by MGM's gilt-edged George Cukor. A few days into shooting, Laughton withdrew from the part of Mr Micawber and was replaced by W.C. Fields. Neither 'creative differences' nor any other, more satisfac-tory, explanation was ever given for Laughton's departure. Cukor felt: 'Laughton's confidence and self-esteem were never very high. Least of all when he began a picture. I'm surprised he didn't walk off more sets ... A lot depended on his relationship with Elsa, at home, and her opinion of his latest role. He allowed her to have a great emotional sway over him.

'Elsa herself displayed little or no stage fright. She always seemed to have the feeling, about a new project or role, that she had nothing to lose. Elsa knew that what she did, she did very well. Within her own range, she was marvellous. But she was very easy to stereotype.'

It was Cukor who formally introduced me to Lanchester, at his Cordell Drive mansion in the Hollywood Hills. A few years before, I had phone-interviewed her, at some length, upon the release of *Murder By Death*, a 1976 murder mystery spoof. When I brought up the interview, at Cukor's house, Elsa laughed, 'Dear boy, I remember my films, and most of my co-stars, but very, very few of my interviews. The secret to long life,' she whispered, 'is a faulty memory and the constitution of an ox, both of which I'm glad to say I possess!' We subsequently met many times, usually at an English restaurant in Santa Monica which she much favoured – 'Best tea and scones in town!'

In 1935, also at MGM, Elsa had a small role in *Naughty Marietta* with Nelson Eddy and Jeanette MacDonald. 'I don't think I'm the first to spill the beans about Jeanette and Nelson not getting along very well. That, of course, was their business. But it made things very tense on the set, which was already dark with the shadow of Louis B. Mayer, aka Louis B. *Merde*. He personally oversaw all the Eddy and MacDonald musicals, which were the favourites of his films.'

After moving to Universal for *The Bride of Frankenstein* and her biggest role yet, Elsa finished out the year in Britain, fourth-billed in René Clair's comedy classic, *The Ghost Goes West*. She played a Miss Shepperton, said to be named after London Films' major rival, Shepperton Studios. A haughty party guest, she didn't show up – billing notwithstanding – until the very last scene in the film.

'Korda produced. Charles was supposed to star, and at the last minute couldn't, owing to some technical Hollywood hitch. So Korda got Robert Donat to play the ghost and his descendant, and also got stuck with me – *I* didn't have a hitch! Naturally, he gave me the smallest possible role. Once again. This is where a bad memory comes in handy. I only wish mine were worse!'

Elsa did not make another American film until 1941. It wasn't her first prolonged spell of relative inactivity. She remained vital to Laughton's career and interests, and dabbled in theatre, nightclubs and a *salon* which attracted a transatlantic admixture of more or less eccentric actors, painters, poets and Laughton-admirers. Being 'la Laughton', as Louella Parsons sometimes called her, was nearly a full-time job, '*if* I let it be, and I usually did. Why not? It was typically fun and colourful and gay – in both senses of the word!'

The down-side was playing moon to Laughton's sun. She

philosophized, 'Being known as Mrs Somebody may have been more of a detriment than a plus. I'm not sure. Even then, I tried to visualize life or acting as it might have been without Charles. But my best roles were often opposite him … I don't want to sound ungrateful or bitchy, and what's the use of speculating about what might have been? A good imagination is practically as detrimental to one's health as a good memory,' she giggled.

One of the couple's best vehicles was the then underrated *Vessel of Wrath* (US: *The Beachcomber*) by W. Somerset Maugham. The 1938 picture, Elsa's first since *Rembrandt*, starred the twosome as an alcoholic loafer and a religious spinster who battle, then befriend, each other. He ultimately confesses that his father was a clergyman and she discloses that her father was alcoholic. A charming and offbeat love story, it was set in the South Seas, and was the first offering from Laughton's own company.

Unfortunately, like the quietly paced *Rembrandt*, *Vessel* was a commercial flop. 'It was non-sensationalistic, and all the *more* so after the Breen Office [the censors] yanked out any scenes with sexual connotations,' Lanchester half-fumed, the recollection still vivid. 'If you have a story set in the South Seas, the censors are always convinced that it is rife with sexual connotations and immorality!'

Miss Jones, the sparring partner of beachcomber Ginger Ted, was one of the actress's favourite roles. 'She experiences real character development. She begins as cold and self-righteous, yet after she gets to know Ginger Ted and learns of his past and his amorous adventures, she yields up a great sympathy and understanding for him. He, in turn, melts her – for want of a better word – frigidity.' Elsa could as easily have been describing her and Laughton's un*reel* life.

'My sole objection to the movie is its ending. Character development is one thing, but character reversal is another.' *Vessel*'s finale finds the fun-loving ex-Miss Jones, heretofore an avid anti-alcoholic, running a local pub with her husband, called the Fox and Rabbit!

'Other than the ending, I think *The Vessel of Wrath* is one of our best pieces of work together, and in its own way a classic. Like *The African Queen*, which it resembles.'

Also in 1938, Elsa spearheaded a joint publicity effort in the form of a book, *Charles Laughton and I*. 'About two lovable Limey eccentrics, allegedly joined at the hip.' In the 1970s, she contributed a foreword to Charles Higham's Laughton biography in which she publicly revealed her late husband's homosexuality, and in 1983 she published her autobiography, *Elsa Lanchester, Herself*, in which she satisfied her fans' ongoing requests for details about the shooting of *The Bride of Frankenstein*.

Despite *Vessel of Wrath*'s commercial failure, the acting couple never considered stopping working together, on screen or stage. Most critics felt their stage work was superior to their joint film work. Among their memorable stage collaborations: *Mr Prohack*, *Payment Deferred* – Lanchester did not feature in the screen version – *The Tempest* – with her as Ariel and he as Prospero – and *Peter Pan*, with Captain Hook played by the alter ego of Captains Bligh and Kidd. Elsa was the last Peter Pan personally selected by playwright James Barrie.

'Barrie hadn't wanted Charles to play Captain Hook. He thought Charles would frighten the littler children, because of his "screen gallery of grotesques", as he called them. This hurt Charles very deeply, especially since Barrie was, as he put it, "one of the brotherhood".

'We played *Peter Pan* in London, but then I had to tour in the provinces without Charles. He was due to make a film [the uncompleted *I, Claudius*]. What that meant was a great dip in the box office. I didn't mind about the money; I've never been very materialistic. But it meant we got far less attention, and the play had a shorter, less glorious run.'

On film, with a few exceptions, the pair's collaborations were low-key and oddly disappointing: *Tales of Manhattan*, 1942, *Forever and a Day*, 1943, and *The Big Clock*, 1948 (remade in 1987 as *No Way Out*). 'Charles was at his best playing larger-than-life characters, for *he* was larger-than-life. I could then react to *him*, and even match him at times … In the vast majority of my roles, I wasn't active, I was reactive, and so the result, the chemistry, really depended on who I was acting with … If Charles had a poor role, I didn't shine either.'

In *Clock*, Laughton was a white-collar murderer (in the remake, said murderer was depicted as homosexual!). 'He played a malevolent businessman, which was a gigantic stretch! Charles was worried, but I told him, "If I can play a domestic or nanny, you can play a true-to-life businessman!" '

Laughton biographers Simon Callow and Charles Higham have noted that it was he who wanted offspring, his wife who put her foot down. Elsa may have made convincing nannies and domestics in family pictures like *Lassie Come Home* and *Son of Fury*, but she was seldom – if ever, indeed – cast as a mother. She also explained, 'My parents were somewhat aghast with certain of my roles, since they didn't hold with the idea that one class of people should be subservient to, or serve, others.'

As to her almost background roles in those future family classics: 'Never try to compete with a dog, horse, child or any other form of lovable animal life. It's a thankless job, unless you like to take the money and run. Alas, I didn't really start getting very choosy until my old age!'

Upon moving to Hollywood, Lanchester discovered that she had escaped England's class system for a rigid caste system. 'I repeatedly had tiny roles in very good movies, like Edmund Goulding's *The Razor's Edge* (1946), from the novel by Maugham. Alas, I did more watching than acting. Big stars on beautiful sets, speakingly highly literate words … For, the truth is, Hollywood is the most undemocratic town on earth.

'Stars only mix with other stars, and there is a definite pecking order. I only managed to transgress that order –

when I chose to – because of my marriage to Charles. He was a very big star in both senses of the word!'

Insiders said the marriage was marred by increasing bickering over the years, sharpened by Elsa's tongue. 'It's the Irish in me,' she told Christopher Isherwood, who was preparing an unrealized play about Socrates for Laughton. In time, Elsa admitted her sore feelings about 'the Oscar situation. Charles won one, and appeared in several Oscar-nominated roles and movies. I only got two supporting nominations, won neither, and the first was for one of my treacliest roles!'

She was first nominated in 1949 for the nun story *Come to the Stable*, starring Loretta Young. 'What I said about animals and children goes double for nuns! Don't ever play a nun, unless she's a novice, a Mother Superior or Loretta Young. I know people who have seen that movie two or three times, and don't even remember me in it!

'The thing is, in the old days, it wasn't like now. If you were off the screen for as long as two years, the movie people assumed you had retired or moved to Kathmandu. Sometimes, you just took a role to keep your hand in …'

The 1957 *Witness For the Prosecution* resulted in nominations for both Elsa and Charles – he, for Best Actor – and was the effervescent culmination of their celluloid partnership. Fittingly, they depicted humorous but persistent adversaries who through it all nurtured an underlying affection, or need, for each other. 'In the nicest sense of the phrase,' volunteered Elsa, 'all our scenes together were love scenes.'

Billy Wilder, director of the brilliant adaptation of Agatha Christie's play, said of Elsa, 'She was one of the two most original actors I ever worked with, the other being Charles Laughton.' Miss Plimsoll, her relentlessly fussy though winning nurse-cum-nanny, remains Lanchester's finest screen creation. Even as accomplished an actress as Deborah Kerr could not approach Elsa's comic heights in the part, when *Witness* was remade for television.

'Charles and I initially had grave doubts about joining *Witness*. He was intimidated by Tyrone Power, who was a close friend of his but a daunting screen Presence with a capital P. And I was intimidated by Marlene Dietrich, who was not a friend, though she greatly admired Charles, and who was another of those supra-luminary legends. Then Wilder pointed out that we would be 'balanced' by the other two stars. He said that in most of our films together, Charles and I were either too foreign or too overpowering – or both – for American audiences.

'In this case, he turned out to be absolutely right! And it even turned out that Ty Power and Marlene had been somewhat intimidated about working with us! Fancy that!'

Separately from Laughton, Elsa had a semi-active career in live entertainment. 'I could have performed with him more, and he was quite protective, but I didn't care for the constant comparisons people made.' Simon Callow has written, 'It is not clear to what extent Laughton tried to promote her, but the very fact that she would need "promotion" must have been unbearable to her.'

Many observers believed that as a dramatic actress, Lanchester was lacking. On the other hand, she rarely got anything but comical or wry roles. She was compared to 'an off-colour Joyce Grenfell,' and was once described as 'Bea Lillie without the genius'. Had Laughton or James Whale not come along, it is likely that Elsa would have held more firmly to theatrics. 'More than anything, I like applause,' she stated after completing her final film, the 1980 *Die Laughing*.

Thus, when middle age mandated even fewer screen parts, Elsa co-founded the Turnabout Theatre, known from 1941 to 1956 as Los Angeles' 'bohemian hangout'. She performed there regularly, and developed a one-woman act with musical accompaniment with which she toured during and after Laughton. Her trademark song was the quaintly suggestive 'When a Lady Has a Piazza'.

'I was fond of being able to devise my own material and

have a hand in what went on at our little cabaret spot. Unlike filming, where you've scarcely any input and everything's so pat and bland ... Unfortunately, because of my association with the Turnabout group, Hollywood at first thought I was no longer fit to do movies, or had lost all interest in them!'

After *Witness For the Prosecution*, Elsa played a witch named Queenie in the 1958 *Bell, Book and Candle*, from John Van Druten's slyly feline play. 'It was great fun, very relaxed. Kim Novak was very easy to work with. She didn't have the typical star ego or condescensions.'

Elsa was then away from the screen until 1964, partly owing to Charles's protracted bout with cancer and the aftermath of his death in 1962. 'We had our ups and downs, but we were best friends, and when he was gone, I was so disoriented ...

'I was lucky my "type" was being requested by the Disney studios.' In between such period flicks as *Honeymoon Hotel* and *Pajama Party*, she found employment in Disney fare like *Mary Poppins*, 1964, *That Darn Cat!*, 1965, and *Blackbeard's Ghost*, 1967. 'The Disney people were a bit stodgy, and the pay wasn't the best in town, but they treated their stars well, and they liked to use you again and again. They liked knowing what they could expect from you.

'It was lovely working on *Mary Poppins*. The atmosphere was almost like being back in London, at the turn of the century. Or, rather, what I *imagined* the turn of the century to be like ... I could only have hoped that my part were bigger, and perhaps a bit less cantankerous' (she played a crotchety, pre-Poppins nanny). 'I don't mind so much, playing nags and scolds, but then the public assumes that's what I'm like!'

She worked relatively little in television, but in 1969 did a telefilm titled *In Name Only*, and was seen in the feature *Me, Natalie* with Patty Duke. 'I thought it was a delightful and innovative film. Patty played an unattractive but charming girl; they put buck teeth on her. But once again, I had a small, small part. I was a bohemian landlady in a building that Natalie moves into, and I point out two young gay men and say, 'Don't they make a lovely couple?' Well, that's true enough to life, for living in, or near, Hollywood, most of my male friends have been gay.

'But when I viewed *Me, Natalie*, I was terribly disappointed. All my scenes but the one on the staircase had been cut! An acquaintance of mine who saw the film really got my dander up. She said, 'Elsa, why do you take on such tiny roles? You must love seeing your name in the credits.' What some people fail to realize is that nobody who is established takes on a tiny role. Instead, they shoot several scenes with you, and then the director and editor hack the scenes to bits. So you end up looking silly, with two or three minutes out of an entire motion picture!

'Regarding credits, I couldn't care less about those, or seeing my name in lights. I stopped caring about credits after *The Bride of Frankenstein*.'

In 1971 she undertook the rat-hit *Willard*. 'I don't have much of an excuse for that one, except that it was a first of its kind, and I always like to try something completely, mind-bogglingly new.' Then came 1973's *Terror in the Wax Museum*, a comedy-horror with Ray Milland. Elsa impersonated a greedy proprietress who finds that ghoulish murders at her wax museum are definitely improving business.

In 1976 she did a take-off on mystery sleuth Jane Marple, as Miss Jessica Marbles in Neil Simon's *Murder By Death*, helmed by ex-actor Robert Moore. 'Bobby made it such fun, it was the best time I'd had in years! I worked with Estelle Winwood, who played my antiquarian nurse, and we caught up on all the gossip since 1954,' when they'd filmed *The Glass Slipper*.

'Estelle is one of the few people as free-spirited as me. Her façade is very prim and even somewhat gothic, but she's a merry old soul, and we always laugh together. She has the most wonderful stories, not just about Tallulah Bankhead, but about everyone she's worked with or known. Working with Estelle and all the others was a wonderful comeback for me.'

Murder By Death's success was greatly abetted by its cast: Alec Guinness, Truman Capote, Maggie Smith, David Niven, Peter Sellers, James Coco, Peter Falk ... 'I was rather hoping they'd do a sequel,' giggled Elsa. 'Or else consider me to play Miss Marple in a few of those Christie things.' Sadly, it was her last substantial role, although she lived another decade. Her final years were spent, like so many others,' at the Motion Picture & Television Country Home & Hospital in Woodland Hills, California.

'For the past several years, I've deliberately turned down roles. Refusals all over the place! I was fortunate to still get offers, and a few of the very young producers or directors who have contacted me told me how much they loved my work in *Bride* or other movies. But I turned down roles, less for reasons of health or laziness than for reasons of good taste. And I'm no prude, either. Most of the things I was offered were in the horror genre, but it was no longer psychological or stylish horror, as in the 1930s and 1940s.

'This kind of horror is the kind you hear of on the news or read about in the papers – bloody, sickening violence. I didn't want to be a party to that, or even to betray the memory of James Whale, who made such classy and timeless films. So I've simply worked far less, if at all, because no one ever offers me just a straightforward grandmotherly sort of role! Oh, well.'

In the 1920s, *Vogue* magazine wrote, 'Her hair is in the chestnut trees of London and her feet are in the mud of the Thames.' Long, long after that, she granted that 'I'd always wanted attention. *Craved* it. I deliberately kept my hair wild-looking, to attract it. Then I gradually discovered that my hair was naturally unruly!

'Similarly, I took up pants for shock value. In Hollywood I was told that no proper actress would wear pants in public – unless she had the sex appeal of a Dietrich! For a time, I complied. But soon I found that pants were far more comfortable! So I stopped caring about false propriety.'

As for losing most contact with England during the second half of her life, she emphatically shook her head. 'I didn't give it up. Wherever I was was, for a time, England. Friends would ask why I didn't go back more often, or work there, after I wasn't getting very good roles in Hollywood. I just told them that I was too old to travel! The truth is, when I discovered California, I discovered – and indulged – my lazy streak. I didn't fight for roles, and I didn't take maximum advantage of being a big star's wife.

'Looking back, I don't mind. I've met actresses more famous and awarded than myself, who privately spend their lives telling anyone who will listen how they missed out and were betrayed along the way. I have very few regrets, if any. I just enjoyed living my life, even if it wasn't in the dead centre of the spotlight.'

Summing up her career, she remarked, 'Laughter was never very far away. I simply entertained people as best I could. I don't think I could have asked more of myself than that, for although I didn't work as often as some, whenever I did, I gave it my all. And if my characters tended strongly to resemble me, my only explanation is that, from the very start, I've had a very strong personality!'

One British reviewer found it appropriate that 'her autobiography ends with an exclamation mark, for much about Elsa Lanchester, her life and characters, has been surprising. In her goggle-eyes one always discerns an incipient titter. The actress herself is a sort of human exclamation mark!'

7

Beatrice Lillie

In London in 1970 I went to a party. It was a celebrity party, and I was able to go thanks to my grandfather, who was in the Diplomatic Service in England right after the war. At the party, I met Sir Cecil Beaton, who introduced me to Sir Robert Helpmann, who knew John Philip Huck, who was Beatrice Lillie's live-in aide and, after 1977, her guardian. It was through Huck that, in 1972, I was able to interview Lillie. But it was contingent upon my also interviewing him afterwards, so he might correct any 'misinformation' she gave about herself. I've not included any of Mr Huck's comments here.

'I was born in the Gay Nineties (1894) in Toronto. Victoria was on her throne, and Mumsie was frequently on her high-horse, for she had a very talented daughter – my older sister Muriel … When Muriel got a booking, Mumsie would try and make it a family act. We were in fact the Lillie Trio.'

'Mumsie' was Lucy Shaw, a distant relative of George Bernard and a sometime concert singer. Bea's father John was a civil servant – 'usually more civil than Mumsie, who

101

was a human cataclysm when she had to be'.

For a time, the Lillie Trio were booked by Colonel Cornell of Cobourg, Ontario. The millionaire sponsored amateur theatricals, and his granddaughter Katharine became a close friend of Bea's. The tomboy of the family had a razor-sharp wit, and while Muriel was making progress as a concert pianist, Bea aimed to become a comedienne during an era when it was not thought possible for a female to earn a living via humour.

Bea befriended what biographer Bruce Laffey called 'butch young comediennes', some of whom remained lifelong friends. Another chum was actress Hope Williams, whose closely cropped hair had caused much comment. Hope gave Bea professional advice and eventually urged her to cut her own hair, which she did, later softening the look with her trademark pillbox. 'I wore them *aeons* before Jackie Kennedy,' sniffed Lillie.

Bea had initially wanted to sing for her supper, thus following in her mother's footsteps. 'I sang for the masses, when I could locate them. But my reactions to lovey-dovey lyrics were amusing to said masses, so I learned to blend comedy and song.' When she went out on her own, she sometimes billed herself as Bey-a-tree-chay (the Italian pronunciation of Beatrice), the 'mezzanine soprano'. During the First World War, she sang to the troops such down-home pleasers as 'Michigan,' 'Lazy' and 'Susannah's Squeaking Shoes', the latter co-written by Muriel.

In 1913 Lucy Lillie took Muriel to London to advance her career. The next year, 'wee perwerse Bea' joined them, while John stayed in Canada and sent money. In 1914, the youngest Lillie made her professional stage début, but success did not prove instantaneous. 'They had to get used to me, and then they had to discover me.' Already twenty-ish, Bea was surprised to find herself frequently cast as a male impersonator in sketches and revues. For instance, the song 'When I Said Goodbye', sung as a soldier. And 'My River Girl', in which she perched on a bike dressed as an Eton schoolboy: 'I had on bicycle clips, a coat and cap, and was mistaken more than a few times for a chap!'

Bea bided her time, but in 1920 married, thus achieving headlines at last. The bridegroom was Sir Robert Peel, a baronet and descendant of the Prime Minister after whom British policemen were nicknamed 'bobbies'. The two, said insiders, had little in common besides ambition. Robert, who had grown up bored and rudderless, craved some of Bea's showbiz glamour, while she was not averse to prestige and a title.

A gambler, Peel had little money, and lost most of what he had. Bea continued her career out of both desire and necessity. In fact, for most of their marriage, the couple lived apart. Bea's biographer revealed that the bills for the birth of their son Robert in 1920 were footed by her platonic gay friend Ivor Novello. And it was Lucy who brought up the future baronet. Bea herself never learned to cook, sew, garden or keep house. (Interestingly, she never met her mother-in-law, who was reportedly scandalized that her son had married an actress.)

Bea's professional breakthrough was *André Charlot's London Revue of 1924*, with which she also travelled to New York. Her stage antics were becoming notorious and celebrated, such as finishing a torch song by hiking up her gown and exiting the spotlight on hitherto hidden roller-skates; twirling a long strand of pearls about her neck, hula-hoop-style, then yawning elaborately; and singing such splendid nonsense as 'Wind 'Round My Heart', 'Three Little Fishies', 'Maud' (co-written by Muriel) and her signature tune, 'There Are Fairies At the Bottom of Our Garden'.

In 1926 the Charlot revue took Bea, her bosom buddy Gertrude Lawrence and Jack Buchanan to Hollywood. 'At the end of the show, Valentino and several other stars came up on stage with us, welcoming us Brits to Tinseltown. It was a night of glamour and dreams.' In America, Bea's shorn hair was advertised in department stores as the Eton Crop and caught on with flappers across the land. 'My hair was considered very boyish, my beads girlish and my demeanour pixie-ish!'

The pioneering comedienne would come to be an inspiration if not exactly a role model to successors like Joan Rivers and Lily Tomlin. Despite their vastly differing styles, as Rivers put it, 'What other woman can you name who was out there being funny, being successful and becoming rich?' Tomlin asserted, 'She was unconventional ... She refused to be limited by her gender or by the roles she was routinely handed.'

Ironically, for a long time André Charlot insisted on presenting Lillie as a 'girl hero' in top hat, white tie and tails. In revues like *Samples* and *Some*, she was the man-about-town nostalgically longing in song to go back to, say, Canada or some other less harried spot. But in 1917, in *Cheep*, Bea improvised and proved she could be funny regardless of her apparel or apparent gender. In Act II, as a member of the Dedleigh Dull Quartette, she attempted, in a green satin gown, an artsy love ballad titled 'Bird of Love Divine'.

At the same time, she had a bouquet of chrysanthemums protruding from her *décolletage*, and during the second verse, when she tired of holding the sheet music, she propped it up on the serviceable flowers, further convulsing her audience. 'I usually kept a straight face ... What I did not do was burlesque or slapstick.' From then on, Charlot allowed Lillie to include feminine attire in her on-stage wardrobe.

Also in 1926, Bea made her movie début in *Exit Smiling*. She played a gent with a moustache opposite Doris Lloyd; their flirtation scene was risqué for its day. The film co-starred fellow Torontian Mary Pickford's brother Jack in his penultimate picture – he died at thirty-seven – and in his screen début, character comic Franklin Pangborn.

Oddly, Lillie's film career was to be a brief and unshining thing. She did eight and a half films – one was a short – and the two most popular by far were her last, but not necessarily because of her presence. 'I could say that celluloid is only for pretty cardboard figures, or that my fans prefer to see me in the flesh, not as shadows on a screen,' she said in 1966, the year she made her last movie, *Thoroughly Modern Millie*.

'But let's face the music, dear. I've had bad luck in pictures. That's all.'

While staying in Hollywood in the late 1920s, Bea resided at the fabled Garden of Allah, the converted house of silent star Alla Nazimova. The hotel's pool was said to be shaped like the Black Sea, in honour of Alla's Russian heritage. Buster Keaton, Bea's neighbour at the Garden, reportedly fell in love with her. But in vain. Said Sheilah Graham, the British Hollywood columnist, 'Bea's passion was directed at Greta Garbo, the first woman she'd ever seen who wore slacks in public.' Director and party-giver George Cukor declared that Lillie was the only person he ever saw make Garbo laugh, at one of his affairs.

In 1928 Bea co-starred with actor-dancer Clifton Webb (he became a movie star in middle age in *Laura*, 1944) in the stage extravaganza *She's My Baby*. One reviewer found her 'too funny for words, so instead I'll lay down my pen and laugh some more, at the memory of her'. Her humour was typically subtle, expressed in song and sketches, increasingly solo. She later insisted, 'I never stood there and told jokes. Oh, nooo!

'I acted. Even when I sang, I was a comic actress ... You know, if my nose had been about a quarter-inch shorter, I might have become a screen siren or a diva.'

Asked her favourite medium, Bea answered, 'Stage. Live people out there! It seems my entire life has been one show after another. You name the year ... ah, but I can't name the show, there have been so many. Once I earned a reputation it wasn't hard to find work. Writers, producers and friends came to me and made marvellous but decent propositions.'

In 1929 Bea returned uneventfully to the screen in the mistitled *The Show of Shows*. In 1930, in the film *Are You There?* she played 'a lady detective who in the course of her uncoverings is an acrobat, a nurse, a masseuse, a horsewoman and a big-game hunter. Fox called it a musical farce. It *was* a farce.' Then she stayed away till 1938, with the Bing Crosby vehicle *Dr Rhythm*. The *New York Times* felt, 'Crosby, Lillie and Company are wooing the old comic muse as though they had a $5 bet on its surrender. Maybe a $3 bet. Nothing quite so grim as their pursuit of the elfin guffaw has been seen in these parts since Martha Raye fell down the incinerator chute.'

As Bea put it, 'Whenever I made a stab at the movies, they stabbed right back!'

Rhythm co-star Stanley Holloway elucidated, 'They don't know how to display Beatrice to best advantage ... They're nervous about funny foreigners, especially a female with a title,' for Bea couldn't escape being Lady Peel (or as comedy-lovers labelled her, Lady Banana Peel). She recalled, 'Certain American promoters, in awe of British titles, took advantage of mine. They misleadingly billed me as "Direct From London & the Palace", as if I'd come from Buckingham Palace, not the Palace Theatre!'

In 1932 Bea made a dramatic change, playing 'for pathos, not pot-holes.' She was a nurse in the New York première of Bernard Shaw's *Too True To Be Good*. So was the notion that she could escape comedy: *Too True* put her back into revues for good. 'Even confirmed Shavians,' she explained, 'were in titters from my allegedly mobile eyebrows or curling lips – come to think of it, my entire and inherent demeanour!'

When I wondered if the 'female Chaplin' had ever pined for a given dramatic role or yearned to be known for her versatility, she waggled her head sideways and rolled her eyes heavenwards. 'Regrets, I've had a few – about my personal life. Marrying for the wrong reason ... Minor matters like that. Now, if I'd remained anonymous, *that* I'd have regretted!

'If you become the person you're meant to be, and if you do it in public and entertain said public, then you'll have success. And as long as the public keeps coming to see you, what real regrets could you devise? If I'd been wondrous as "Camille", I wouldn't have been a riot at comedy – hell, I wouldn't have been *me*, and then where would I be?'

'I've always had a funny mind,' said Lillie in 1972. 'I poked fun at convention and pretence.' (Said Kenneth Tynan, 'Her title sits on her like a halo on an anarchist.') After a heavy pause, she added, 'I don't know what I'd have done without mine ...' Sense of humour, she no doubt meant. If Mae West was the most quoted woman in America, Queen Bea was the most quoted – in mixed company too – in Britain. She became famous for her witticisms and retorts, and was the subject of innumerable showbiz stories, some of them apocryphal.

A few Bea-attitudes:

– Once in a London taxi, Bea's Pekingese went pee-pee on the back seat. After the cab driver saw what had happened, he berated the star loud and long for her pet's bad manners. Bea was beside herself with anger ('Such language, and in front of the dog!'). So she paid the man, got out of the cab, glared at him and announced, '*I* did it!'

– At a formal New York reception, Bea was introduced to Josephine Baker. The black American who had become a star in 1920s Paris was behaving very grandly, even affecting a French accent. Baker extended a gloved hand as though expecting it to be kissed, and confessed what a 'great *plaisir*' it was to meet 'Lady Peel'. Bea smiled, firmly shook Josephine's hand, and drawled, 'Ah likes you too, honey.'

– Noël Coward, who always called her Beattie, was informed about a new male comic who was being described in the press as 'a masculine Beatrice Lillie'. Coward snapped, 'Don't be redundant!' When told, Bea was highly amused.

– Another time, Noël commented disapprovingly about a masculine tailored suit Bea was wearing. 'You look almost like a man.' She hissed back, 'So do you!' Then they laughed, shook hands and swapped their tailors' addresses.

– The friends were in Paris together, staying in adjacent

hotel rooms. Bea coyly asked Noël, 'Do you have a gentleman in your room?' He answered, 'Just a minute – I'll ask him.'

– Upon checking into the Château Marmont Hotel in Hollywood, Bea entered her name in the register as Lady Peel. The young woman at the desk read it and enthusiastically demanded, 'Are you really a lady?' Heads turned, and Bea shouted back, 'You're goddamned right!' then swept out.

– Bea often invited up platonic male friends to her London or New York apartment. Once, a bachelor producer she'd assumed was gay invited her to his place. 'For a *nightcap*, he said. Well! It wasn't until he produced a bottle of champagne and the nightcap to go with it that I finally caught on!'

– On the Jack Paar Show, Bea told the true story of an elderly lady friend who had received a phone call from Western Union, then insisted that as she'd never in her life received a singing telegram, the message should be sung to her. The exasperated caller finally agreed to sing her the telegram, and began, 'Your sister Rose is dead ...'

– One of Bea's lifelong friends was the globular and terminally plain café society hostess Elsa Maxwell. Elsa was once described as resembling William Frawley of *I Love Lucy* fame. When a reporter solicited Bea's candid opinion of Miss Maxwell, she offered, 'Elsa? Oh, she's just another pretty face.'

– Bea once called her friend Anna Russell, the Aussie satirist, 'the down-under diva', and was amazed to find that her remark had been censored from a TV talk show!

– At a Buckingham Palace dinner party, a nervous or clumsy waiter spilled soup down Beatrice Lillie's formal gown. The waiter turned to stone until Bea waved him away after exclaiming, 'Never darken my Dior again!'

– At another ritzy soirée, a society matron was questioning whether Bea's celebrated pearls were real. The matron could not believe that a mere comedienne could afford a long strand of genuine pearls, and offered to test Bea's with her teeth. Bea smiled, 'But m'lady, surely you're old enough to know that you can't test real pearls with false teeth ...'

– An American fan, at a party, inquired if Lady Peel had a

coronet. 'No, I don't.' The fan shook her head: 'That's a pity. I thought everyone noble had a coronet ...' To which Bea replied, 'My dear, what would I do with a coronet? I wouldn't even know how to play it.'

– At yet another party, a dowager was boasting about her jewellery collection. She explained that she cleaned her diamonds with ammonia, her rubies with Bordeaux, her emeralds with Danzig brandy and her sapphires with milk. Bea stifled a yawn. The dowager then turned to ask, 'How do you clean yours, Miss Lillie?' The comedienne confided, 'Oh, I don't bother cleaning mine. When they gets dirty, I simply throws them away.'

– Jack Buchanan, a Charlot regular, often used to rib Bea about her professional cross-dressing. Backstage one night at the Prince of Wales Theatre, in front of the boys, he asked her, 'On which side do you dress?' She failed to understand, and he asked again. Suddenly, it dawned on her what he meant, and she laughed, 'Why, in Number Five, of course. Stage left.'

– In Chicago one day, Bea and some of the chorus girls in her show went to Elizabeth Arden's. Under the hair-drier, Bea heard a snooty female voice at the desk: 'Oh, if I'd known there would be chorus girls here today, I never would have come.' When Bea finished, Mrs Armour – of the meat-packing company – was still waiting for her appointment. Bidding *adieu* to the manager, Bea loudly proclaimed, 'You may tell the butcher's wife that Lady Peel has finished.'

While living off-and-on in New York in the 1930s, Bea was asked by an American reporter why she did not simply divorce her always absent husband. She let her secretary-companion Sadie Walsh handle the question. 'Walshie' replied, 'Getting a divorce in London is comparable to signing your own death warrant. And we did so enjoy the interview ...' In her memoirs, Bea allowed, 'I had become what may be described as a bachelor lady, with a long-distance son to care for.'

Her East End regular guests included Noël Coward, Ivor

Novello, Helen Hayes, Harpo Marx, Elsa Maxwell, Alec Woollcott, Lady Mendl, and above all, her best friend (and former understudy) Gertie Lawrence, with whom she lived for years on 54th Street. The two highly ambitious women got along swimmingly, for they never competed: Lawrence dispensed glamour via drama, and Lillie merriment via mirth. Said Lawrence, 'We're practically Siamese twins, or so people say, but hardly identical.'

In 1934 Bea's estranged husband died of peritonitis at thirty-six. A friend much later inquired whether she and Peel would have stayed together had he lived? 'God, no.' Her son Robert Peel became the sixth and last baronet of the line. He was killed in action during the Second World War in Ceylon. Bea's sometime friend Estelle Winwood stated, 'Bea's work carried her through her misfortunes … After her son died, her humour became a little more heartfelt, yet it became more difficult to befriend her.'

So, the comedienne forged ahead, alternating Broadway and the West End, Coward and Novello, for example, Coward's *This Year of Grace* and *Set To Music* (featuring 'Marvellous Party') and Novello's *March With Me*. Her hits included *The Third Little Show* (introducing 'Mad Dogs and Englishmen'), *At Home Abroad* ('Get Yourself a Geisha' and 'Paree'), *The Show Is On* with Bert Lahr, and *Inside U.S.A.*

Richard Haydn, her co-star in the 1939 *Set to Music*, noted, 'She isn't the sort that's always asking for new material. She can do the latest stuff, and jolly well, but she'll re-polish an old routine till it sparkles like crystal and becomes a classic. Only she can do what she does.'

In 1943 Bea returned to the screen, starring with actor-director Clive Brook and Googie Withers in an adaptation of Frederick Lonsdale's play *On Approval*. It concerns a rich and impossible woman who decides to holiday chastely in Scotland with her intended fiancé until she finds out if he is really suitable for her. In its heyday, *On Approval* was deemed adults-only fare. But the movie was too Victorian for wartime England and too English for America, and quietly flopped.

A watery Beatrice Lillie in her last movie, *Thoroughly Modern Millie*, 1967. (*Doug McClelland*)

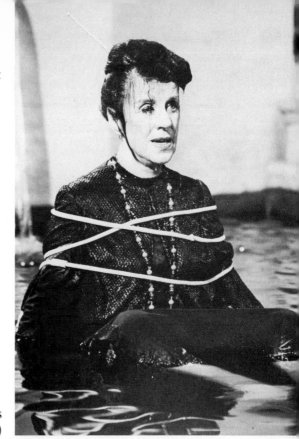

Lillie on Broadway in Noël Coward's *High Spirits*, 1965. (*Doug McClelland*)

Rachel Roberts and Richard Harris in *This Sporting Life*, 1962.

Roberts, Sir John Gielgud, Wendy Hiller and cast in *Murder on the Orient Express*. (*Doug McClelland*)

In 1944 Bea was back on stage in Cole Porter's *Seven Lively Arts*. The composer affirmed, 'She has the most loyal following of almost anyone I know, definitely so among those who create laughter. She is all but worshipped.'

Bea explained, 'After the war and entertaining troops around the world and becoming ill countless times without complaint, I decided to be less of a workhorse. I became slightly more discriminating about what I would do. I'd become more accustomed to big productions, and to tell you the truth, I began thinking, "Why shouldn't I do a show all by my lonesome?" How often I was thrust into a show along with other stars, the philosophy being that there would be something for everyone.'

As her following grew, there was enough demand for a one-woman show, which was then a fairly new concept. Thus, after more star-bespangled productions, mostly on Broadway, and a barely released 1949 movie, she opened in 1952 in *An Evening With Beatrice Lillie*. 'I'd had a few fleeting doubts,' she apprised me. 'I knew I had the very best of fans, but I'd never got around to taking a head-count. And to some folks, it's true, I'm an acquired taste – like anchovies or chow mein.'

The Praise-Bea vehicle enjoyed thousands of performances. After a year at the Booth Theatre, it toured the US and Britain and Ireland. Noël Coward wrote three new numbers for it, and future composer Leslie Bricusse made his acting début in it as the token leading man. *Evening* won Bea a special Tony in 1953 and lasted until 1956, when she made a cameo appearance in the blockbuster hit film, *Around the World in 80 Days*.

'A filmic success at last!' she told the Los Angeles *Times*. 'Am I grateful? You tell me! Am I?' She added that virtually everybody in showbiz 'since Annie Oakley is in the cast, so I'm in good company, though rather stifled.'

Bea increasingly preferred star vehicles; however, she usually accepted commercial realities. 'I could pick between being a small part of a big show or starring in my own somewhat scaled-down show, after the wonderful over-exposure of my one-woman effort.' So she toured in *Beasop's Fables*, but found it tiring, for '*An Evening With Me* had taken a lot out of me. Right after *Beasop*, I was casting about for something a mite less strenuous, even if I didn't have the stage all to myself ... Oh, dear, I *do* sound a tad obnoxious!'

The something less strenuous was the 1957 *Ziegfeld Follies*, the Golden Jubilee Edition. Several stars were cajoled into joining in, among them Tallulah Bankhead, Bea's friend and sparring partner. But Tallu departed the elephantine production during its try-out tour and urged Bea not to come aboard a sinking ship: 'Dahling, it's positively Titanic!' In retrospect, Lillie felt, 'I was persuaded too easily to appear in it,' mostly because of the gold-plated Ziegfeld name. The show ran only 124 performances, not the expected long run, and that chiefly because of advance publicity and Bea's name.

In 1958 Bea's star shone more singularly in *Auntie Mame*. Rosalind Russell left the Broadway smash hit after a year and a half to make the classic film version. Auntie Bea played a month in Manhattan before taking the play to London. The *New York Times*' Brooks Atkinson wrote:

'Her impact goes deeper than clowning. It discovers a tender relationship between the comic beldame and her little nephew. By the time you read this, Miss Lillie will have made *Mame* her own.' The UK *Mame* lasted over a year, and gave Bea the chance to sample home life at Peel Fold, the estate she had bought at Henley-on-Thames soon after the Second World War. Mother Lucy, still vigorous in her eighties, spent her final years at Peel Fold.

After her triumph as 'Auntie Mame', Bea informed the press that Patrick Dennis had been thinking of his aunt as played by la Lillie when he wrote the novel. Likewise, she claimed that P.L. Travers modelled her 'Mary Poppins' on her, and later said that both characters had been incarnated by Others because their youth had made them more desirable in producers' eyes.

*

Though she lived to the age of ninety-four and almost into the 1990s, Bea Lillie's last professionally active decade was the 1960s. And not that active, at that. There were several reasons: age was one, and the rumours that she was losing her ability to memorize lines. To counter this, she insisted, 'If I'm the so-called Funniest Woman in the World, and they keep saying I am, then it's because I work mostly from memory and not from a script. My humour doesn't come off a printed page.'

Also, according to co-star Billy DeWolfe, 'She's a legend in her own time, not to mention a legend in her own mind.' With the dazzle of *Auntie Mame* behind her, Bea wanted bigger and better projects, and was dismayed to find that backers were often wary of her due to her age and/or the view that hers was a limited, very specialized talent. Plus, she wanted a bigger say than before in anything she consented to do.

Finally, there was John Philip Huck, a youngish man of oversized girth and ego whom she had met in 1949. He was a supporting actor-singer who became her 'dogsbody', or gofer. In return, he had small parts in some of her shows. Off-stage, he played a larger role, gradually gaining more influence over his employer and alienating her friends. He once had a famous row with Noël Coward which put a permanent wedge between Bea and her ex-friend and associate. The increasingly frail Bea made Huck her bodyguard and then her personal representative.

Huck tried to give the impression he was her boyfriend too, and discouraged her from appearing in public without him. He encouraged her to rely on him for all personal and most professional decisions, and to think of herself as a superstar-legend above the rules which applied to co-stars or directors.

In 1964 Bea made her final theatrical appearance, on Broadway, in Noël Coward's *High Spirits*, a musical version of his hit play *Blithe Spirit*. Bea was the psychic medium Madame Arcati, the role so indelibly portrayed on screen (and in London) by Margaret Rutherford and in the New York play by Mildred Natwick. Bea made it known that luckily for her, she'd never seen either performance, so, unimpeded by either woman's characterization, she could proceed with her usual unique interpretation.

The co-stars included Tammy Grimes, then a potential star, who as romantic leading lady featured heavily in the show directed by Noël Coward. It was the third time he directed 'Beattie', and he found, 'She was beyond and above being directed. She had a demon on her shoulder, or at least by her side,' and she and Huck 'nagged and bullied everyone connected with the project into augmenting Arcati's part'.

But as the film classic proves, Arcati is but one ingredient in a complex and soufflé-light treat whose components offset each other. An additional component was the music, and Lillie couldn't always remember her lyrics, though she had demanded extra songs. Plus the fact that a seventy-year-old woman was nightly required not only to ride a bicycle, but sit on and perform from it. The Broadway critics were divided in their estimation of the much-heralded show and of Miss Lillie. Some averred that she was still acting as if she were in a revue, or in a different vehicle from the rest of the cast.

In the limelight again, Bea warmed even to nosier interviewers who asked if she'd ever found a man to replace her late husband. She confided that Coward had wanted her, not Rutherford, for Arcati in the 1940s (he denied it), but that she had been unable, for 'a war and a previous engagement intervened'.

High Spirits was a moderate hit, but by the time it ended, Lillie and Coward were through, and theatrical producers in New York and London were not willing to gamble on her again. Her final venture was *Thoroughly Modern Millie*, a Julie Andrews movie in which Bea played a Eurasian hotel manager who secretly deals in white slavery. The 1920s musical co-starred Carol Channing, but to her complete chagrin, Bea as Mrs Meers – a comic gem of a performance – had not a single song!

A year later, in 1968, Julie Andrews played Gertrude Lawrence in the costly musical *Star!* Bea had considered portraying herself in her best friend's life-story, until producer Saul Chaplin reminded her that the film took Gertie from childhood to 1941, and Lillie was already in her seventies. 'Her spokesman,' said Chaplin, 'had convinced her that she looked twenty or more years younger than her age, and she was already informing us which of her numbers she would be singing in the picture.'

The upshot was that Huck and Lillie refused to permit anyone else to play her in *Star!* and so she was not portrayed or even mentioned in it.

Not long after, at a Museum of Modern Art function in her honour, Bea went up on stage to speak to the audience. Suddenly, a wicked gleam entered her eye, and she announced that she was going to 'show you something you've never seen before ...' and grinningly exposed one of her breasts. She was escorted off stage, and there were conflicting reports that she'd had a recent stroke, was becoming senile or had played a practical joke which had shocked those who regarded her as an institution.

Huck decided she would be best situated at Henley-on-Thames rather than at her Manhattan or London apartments. Friends charged that he was isolating her from city life, transportation and her friends. Estelle Winwood held that 'It's a case of Svengali-ism, the only one I've ever seen. He mesmerized her, and she gave in to his will ... Maybe she saw in him a son who could protect her and ease her old age.

'What he's done isn't to protect her, but to quicken her mental decline. I'm older than she is, and I absolutely know that maturity doesn't mean one goes ga-ga!'

In 1972 Bea published her memoirs. *Every Other Inch a Lady* was written with James Brough but was 'aided and abetted by John Philip' (no surname). The book, a witty read, was also a paean to Philip's talents, 'sacrifices' and prominence in Lillie's latter life. A critic for the LA *Herald*

Examiner wondered, 'Who in heck is John Philip, and why does he intrude so upon an otherwise droll and absorbing autobiography?'

In 1975 Bea suffered a stroke which led to her requiring constant care. A small staff was handpicked by Huck, and fewer friends than ever were allowed access to Peel Fold. In 1977 he got himself appointed her guardian, and she was not seen again by the press. When they inquired after the onceegreat comedienne, he pretended she was in perfect health and right mind though reclusive. In fact, after 1975 she often failed to recognize her closest surviving relatives. Prior to 1975 she'd had spells of mental wanderlust but was usually herself.

'It was her inactivity that eventually severed her connection with reality,' Robert Helpmann told *She* magazine. 'She lived for her work ... When she stopped putting herself in the hands of good directors, when she wanted to see herself solely above the title, she put herself into a position where work eluded her. She had health and energy, but without work to channel these, her mind lost its incentive.'

In 1972, excited by the prospect of a best-seller and *ergo* a comeback, Bea burbled, 'Very soon, I may write a screenplay. About my Pekes. I might star, or just produce it. My little dogs have been such a source of joy and humour to me, and you know, nobody ever went broke with Lassie ...'

But all professional activity was now behind her. If her one unfulfilled goal was a DBE, as some said, it was whispered in theatre circles that Huck had ruined her chances by eschewing all invitations and inquiries from Buckingham Palace. He even wrote back once and scolded the Queen's secretary for not placing his name 'next to Miss Lillie's, aka Lady Peel'.

In early 1989, Beatrice Lillie died of natural causes.
One day later, John Philip Huck died.

8

Rachel Roberts

Ironically, for someone who killed herself at fifty-three,
Rachel Roberts was full of life. During an interview in
between her two 1978 films Foul Play *and* Yanks, *she sat*
in her chair in a Los Angeles hotel room as if poised to jump
or attack. Usually smiling, sometimes frowning or far
away, her responsive tone was emphatic, energetic, a
spectacle. A friend once said, 'Ray was always performing,
always attempting to be the life of the party and the star of
the show – even when there was no show. She just loved
attention. Loathed not having it …'

R achel Roberts was born in Wales in 1927, in Llanelli.
She died in 1980 in Los Angeles. 'My two L's,' she
sarcastically called the two towns. 'I got bored with
one because it was too provincial, too personal. The other
bores me because it's too big and impersonal.'

Rachel's father was a clergyman, her mother a housewife
with a taste for Dickens, Shakespeare and poetry. In her own
words a 'professional Welshwoman', Roberts explained that
her sole English ancestor was her mother's father, a
Shropshire lad who moved into the pits of South Wales and

became a committed socialist. When Rachel was a child, the family moved to Swansea, where school plays provided an outlet for the girl's energy. She particularly enjoyed playing Scrooge:

'The headmaster congratulated me, said I would or could eventually become a fine actress, but not to let it go to my head. But ... I did.'

For a time, nervous asthma put an end to Rachel's budding career.

In 1946 she went to the University of Wales at Aberystwyth, and successfully tried her hand at college plays. 'I did Shakespeare, Shaw, Ibsen ... I thought I was very grand. I did, let's face it, become a snob. I was impressed by my own talent.' Next stop was the Royal Academy of Dramatic Art, in London, in 1948. There, she earned student prizes and stood out – partly because she was older and had been to university. However, to her dismay, graduation did not result in agents' offers of representation. 'I was neither a dainty lass nor a raving beauty,' she explained.

'My time came later, when reality set in. Later, in the 1950s.'

She opened the decade by joining a repertory company in Swansea. 'One year. One uneventful year. I loved Wales, but I longed for England, where acting was more vivid and in demand.' So she left for Stratford-upon-Avon. Also to West Germany to entertain the troops. She read for roles she didn't quite get 'because I was good but not ethereal enough. I was threatening in those days, and the more outwardly masculine the man, the more threatened by a good woman,' she laughed huskily, not without an undertone of anger.

In 1953 she inauspiciously launched a film career with *Valley of Song*, intriguingly titled *Men Are Children Twice* for the American market. Also that year, *The Limping Man* and *The Weak and the Wicked*. Queried about her first movies, Roberts shrugged elaborately, then told me, 'I think it's perfectly true that we create a mental block against negative experiences. Not that those non-vehicles were horrible experiences, nor that I've completely forgotten everything about them. But they were such nothing characters, and I had such high hopes.

'Anyway, they came to nothing. No one remembers my 1950s pictures. The most famous would be *Our Man in Havana*, and few remember me in it!'

In 1955, Rachel all but bullied her way into marriage to actor Alan Dobie – in Swansea, with her father officiating. She had kept proposing to the man, who kept refusing. When she backed off from a marital union, he allowed that neither did he desire an affair with her. Decades later, she reflected, 'The idea of our working together seemed attractive. I thought he could help me ... I was not and am not a loner. I need company. Alan provided company and a secure routine.'

But once married, the two were frequently apart, working and touring. Once she had Dobie in her legal sphere, Roberts turned to affairs with other men, admitting in the 1970s that she had seldom been faithful. 'The best times were when we saw old movies together, or ate together or walked together ... What I'd really wanted was a friend. A male friend – because a male one was just more prestigious and rare than a female one.'

In 1956 Rachel got a break in the form of taking over from Wendy Hiller, who had been taken ill, in *Othello* at the London Old Vic. Her Emilia earned her a solo curtain call. Rachel hoped stardom was around the corner, but not yet. (She departed the Bristol Old Vic because Peter O'Toole was getting the lion's share of attention and praise.) 'I did this and I did that, and you wouldn't have thought it had to gradually dawn on me that the screen could be my express ticket to fame.'

In 1960 fame hit with the British New Wave classic *Saturday Night and Sunday Morning*. Adapted by Alan Sillitoe from his novel, it put a magnifying glass to the sexual frustrations of the working class, it made an anti-hero star of

Albert Finney, launched Czech-born Karel Reisz's directorial career, and afforded Roberts a plum part as a wife who
becomes pregnant after a secret affair. The Welsh actress got
the part after Diana Dors declined it. It was the type of
star-making but drab and secondary part that most
established stars would shun.

Roberts won the British Academy Award for it in 1961,
while Finney was deemed the most promising newcomer
and the film itself won as best picture. In 1978, Rachel
dourly recalled, 'It was to me a double mystery. For a year or
more after that, I received no offers for more pictures.
Concurrently, Albert, the new kid on the block, went from
strength to strength, and soon after, with *Tom Jones* became
a bona fide star. If he hasn't quite remained a major star, it's
been through his own choice.

'I was never given that choice. The one mystery, you see,
is sexism. The other mystery – still unsolved – is why so long
before another offer. I didn't have my current "difficult"
reputation yet.'

However, in 1960 Rachel Roberts entered a new phase of
her life; one dominated by established star Rex Harrison. It
was at the Royal Court Theatre. Harrison, fifty-two, was
starring in *Platonov*. Roberts was cast as his mistress Anna
Petrovna. The actor, whose stage career had revived with the
musical *My Fair Lady*, had by then been married three
times: to Collette Thomas, Lilli Palmer and Kay Kendall.
Kendall had died prematurely the year before. Palmer had
agreed to divorce 'sexy Rexy' so he could wed his mistress,
who was fatally ill. The agreement was that after Kay died,
Lilli and Rex would re-marry, but by that time, Palmer had
contractually joined with her lover, Carlos Thompson.

Upon the play's closing, Harrison invited Roberts to his
famed villa (alternately shared with Palmer and Thompson)
in Portofino, Italy. If Rex was a bit old to be an ideal lover,
his lifestyle was ideally lush: 'I fell in love with luxury and
with Rex's command of everyone around him. Unlike me,

he seemed always to know how to fulfil his every desire.' Romantic association with the star made a regular of Rachel in the gossip columns, and she basked in the reflected glory.

'With my Alan, it had already ended some time previous to Rex. With Rex in my life, the marriage totally dissolved, like something exposed to bright sunlight.' In 1962, in Genoa, Rachel wed Harrison. She also found a worthy follow-up to *Saturday Night and Sunday Morning*. It was *This Sporting Life*, starring Richard Harris as an anti-heroic rugby player and Roberts as a repressed widow to whom he is drawn. David Storey's screenplay, from his novel, was directed by Lindsay Anderson, who became a lifelong friend. Among the actresses reportedly approached to play Mrs Hammond was Mary Ure. Roberts confessed:

'This woman was repressed. Was masochistic. Was drab and dreary, everything I still think I'm not! I didn't know if I could portray her convincingly. For me, she was a stretch ... Praise me lucky stars I was convinced and convincing. It was my shot, my long-shot, at Oscar!'

Rachel lost the Hollywood Academy Award to Patricia Neal in *Hud*. Though she rued the loss, she was somewhat relieved too, for Harrison had reacted peevishly when she had earlier informed him that she'd won two simultaneous awards, one for *Platonov* plus the British Oscar. 'He wasn't above hitting people – that is to say, slapping women who incurred his displeasure or his rare jealousy. He so rarely had something to be jealous about ...'

Director Karel Reisz revealed, 'Rex was contemptuous of non-star acting. Rex is a star. He puts through his own personality. Whereas Rachel is a very good character actress ... He made her feel she should hold out for star billing ... Rex admired her performances but thought of her films as unglamorous – appearing in dirty clothes as the working classes. It ran counter to his notion of stardom.'

So, for most of the rest of the 1960s, Rachel stayed away from the silver screen on which Rex was shining. She played wife and full-time fan while Harrison went from *Cleopatra*'s

Caesar to the Oscar for Henry Higgins in *My Fair Lady*, a pope in *The Agony and the Ecstasy*, and a glorified vet in the mega-flop *Dr Dolittle*. 'I travelled, I lived it up, I drank.' Among the drawbacks of being the latest Mrs H. were the comparisons with Lilli and Kay. And of Roberts's stalled film career to his flourishing one:

'I was beginning to lose my security that I could pretty well play anything, that I was damned good ... In 1964 I did *Maggie May*, a Lionel Bart musical [in London]. I was solidly happy to be working again, having things go my way for a change. After it was over and we were in Portofino again, the loneliness came back – not exactly ameliorated by the man's growing iciness. He could have sunk the *Titanic* single-handed!'

Though she evinced no lasting interest in having or adopting a child, the actress was mad about animals, particularly cats. But also seals. Once, on a Santa Lucia (in the Caribbean) location for *Dr Dolittle*, she swam into the section of the bay where the trained seals were penned in until required for shooting. She nearly managed to unfasten the net and let the seals escape. The apoplectic producer yelled at Rex Harrison, 'We should have taken out an insurance policy against your wife setting all our animals free!'

In 1968 Rachel returned to the screen. But she was still supporting her husband; she essayed the confidante who schemes with Rex's wife to cure his impotence in the Feydeau farce *A Flea in Her Ear*. Rachel's friend Rosemary Harris played the wife. The movie was a flop on several counts: it added emphasis to *Dr Dolittle* as a sign that Harrison's starring days were over, it dashed Roberts's hopes of picking up her screen career where she'd left off, and it drove an immovable wedge between Rex and Rachel. The wife who had witnessed his greatest celluloid triumphs was now in on the finish of his cinematic prime. Rachel's next screen effort, in 1969, was actually a made-for-TV movie, co-starring Lorne Greene of *Bonanza*. By then she was separated from Harrison, who was being seen with Elizabeth Harris, Richard's wife.

Rachel returned to familiar territory that year by working with ex-husband Alan Dobie in *Who's Afraid of Virginia Woolf?* at the Theatre Royal, Bath. One critic observed, 'Miss Roberts's Celtic fury serves her well as the venomous Martha in this acid-etched portrait of a marriage gone almost fatally sour.'

Settling in Los Angeles more or less for good, Roberts signed with a top talent agency and played a bisexual doctor's wife in the potboiler *Doctors' Wives* (1970). At the time, she was asked if she feared enacting a lesbian character. 'No, should I? Do you mean am I afraid of playing a stereotype?' The reporter's response went unchronicled.

But if Roberts's career was getting back on track, post-Rex, her busy love life was chaotic. She had occasional affairs with male co-workers, she helped support a black hustler, and she became involved with a young Mexican in the fashion industry. Her alcohol-fuelled behaviour at parties was also remarked on. In 1971 she divorced Harrison (who then wed Elizabeth Harris) and appeared in *The Wild Rovers* because she'd had a yen to portray a madam in a saloon.

Her agent Paul Kohner noted, 'Ray is torn between the glitz of Hollywood and the lure of theatrical respectability ... She's a person of many contradictions. More than most of us. Even in this upside-down industry.'

Rachel's first American play was *The Effect of Gamma Rays on Man-in-the-Moon Marigolds*, in Los Angeles. The actress's private insecurities were not allowed to surface in her upbeat portrait of a woman who is essentially a loser. Dan Sullivan of the Los Angeles *Times* wrote, 'The basic objection to Miss Roberts's approach to the part is that she is so damned healthy ... She makes the play almost a romp, moving with gusto, showing us a face radiant with cheer ... The lines say despair, the performer says buck-up!' Roberts played the victim as a victor, said Alexander Walker.

In Britain again, Rachel re-teamed with Albert Finney –

twelve years after *Saturday Night and Sunday Morning* – in the play *Alpha Beta* at the Royal Court. It too was about a self-destructive marriage. The London *Times*' Irving Wardle: '[She] contributes a blank assertion of her marital rights and a view of his extra-marital life that rises from contemptuous indifference to murderous jealousy and threats of suicide when he leaves her.' Rachel won the *Evening Standard*'s Best Actress Award, against Deborah Kerr, Julia Foster, Diana Rigg, and Lauren Bacall.

In 1973 she played a publicist, an Asian vamp, and – ironically – a Welshwoman who commits suicide. These roles occurred in Lindsay Anderson's O *Lucky Man*. Back on stage, she worked for Broadway director Hal Prince in *The Visit*, a heavy Dürrenmatt drama, and *Chemin de Fer*, a Feydeau farce. The roles resulted in a 1974 theatrical first – Roberts was Tony-nominated for both vehicles. That same year, she participated in the all-star *Murder On the Orient Express*. Albert Finney starred as Agatha Christie's Belgian detective Hercule Poirot, Wendy Hiller co-starred as a Russian dowager princess, and Roberts was her German maid.

The rigidly disciplined and unemotional Hildegard Schmidt was in stark contrast to the private Rachel Roberts. *Orient Express* director Sidney Lumet remembered calling Rachel back for a forgotten reaction shot, soon after dismissing the cast for the day. Alas, she was already 'pretty hungover', and terribly ashamed to have her director see her in such a condition. Lumet apologized for the false alarm, pretended nothing was amiss, and shot the close-up the following morning, with the actress professionally sober.

Continuing in her character work, Rachel tackled Dickens in a *Great Expectations* financed by American television. Also in 1975, she co-starred in the film of *Alpha Beta* and in the Australian film *Picnic at Hanging Rock* as Mrs Appleyard, the school headmistress. But important screen roles were fewer and fewer, and stage work occupied only some of the restless Rachel's time. When she landed the continuing role of a judge's housekeeper on *The Tony Randall Show*, she was ecstatic:

'I thought I'd become rich, I'd be happy, I could be a celebrity that everyone on the street recognizes.' In 1977, after a couple of seasons, the TV series ended, with Rachel considerably disillusioned by the small screen. She shortly went into a small but flashy part in what would become a hit movie, *Foul Play*. After its completion, and pending her work in John Schlesinger's *Yanks* (not a hit), we met at the Beverly Wilshire Hotel in Beverly Hills for a 'thirty-minute interview' that lasted almost two hours, and on into my memory.

Q: You've played quiet roles, also very brassy women. Is there any comparison which is more fun to play?

A: Playing the opposite of yourself is difficult. More fun, however! When I was young and far shyer than today, I would have found a harridan a challenge. It's the introvert or the mousy character that's more of a leap, now.

Q: You seem to blend seamlessly into many of your roles. For instance, the Sapphic German lady's-maid in *Murder On the Orient Express*. Is that easy?

A: Not difficult, not easy, but simple. When I was Fräulein Schmidt, I worked from the inside out. As you saw, she was apparently lesbian, probably repressed. Above all, she was in service, dedicated to her princess. A repressed woman, but with vulnerable spots, such as her love for the murdered maid whom you saw in the flashbacks. Then of course we – the costumier and I – worked from the outside in, and between those two methods ... *voilà*: Hildegard Schmidt! (Laughs throatily.)

Q: Is it coincidental that as you've grown older, your roles have grown more unsympathetic?

A: Look, love, I've never been the sympathetic type! They always thought of me for 'problem' roles. But yes, it's the villainess syndrome. Men are not fond of older women! (Laughs.) At least, older men are not. Younger men don't know how to write roles for them. Besides, I'm not retiring or mousy, and I have an alleged accent. Americans take fright at an accent in a woman; if young, she's a temptress, if not young, a villainess. They just take one look at me and hear an earful, and they think 'murderess' or 'stern teacher' or … Hildegard, whom I did not find unsympathetic, but simply Teutonic.

Q: Is it true you play another German in *Foul Play?*'

A: I don't know that it's specified, but she is a villainess, yes (sighs).

Q: What's *Foul Play* about?

A: (Sighs more heavily) It is a starring vehicle for Goldie Hawn and that comedian named after an automobile (Chevy Chase). My character is out to murder the Pope. (Laughs heartily.) The whole time, I was thinking of Rex in *The Agony and the Ecstasy*. Motivation, you know … My character is a big wheel in a tax-the-churches league. Now, that is an idea which gets short shrift but is worth looking into. Seriously.

Q: What is *Yanks* about?

A: Yanks in Britain, during the war. I play a girl's mother (shrugs).

Q: You open up much more than most celebrity interviewees. I wonder you're not on talk shows more often?

A: All they want, after I'm through plugging my new movie, is the ex-Mrs Rex. That's why. It's a shame too – the stories I could tell about that callous bastard! They label you for life, once you've been shackled to somebody famous. Such hypocrites! They love gossip, off-camera, but for the record, they only want to hear nice things. So if I speak the truth, *I* come across as the monster!

Q: Are people still that interested in Rex Harrison?

A: Not *per se*. 'Antique' is a dirty word in America. But the talk show hosts *are* interested in Rex's women – as there have been so bloody many of them.

Q: Is guarding one's privacy more important to British stars?

A: Oh, it's a regular pastime for most of the English! Us

Welsh, we're more honest. Heart on the sleeve, and damn the consequences! Full speed ahead ... But we do have standards. Hollywood's standards are nothing more than Who are you sleeping with now, which is none of their bloody business!

Q: Why do they call him 'sexy Rexy'? I've seen most of his films, and sex appeal is one of the last things he exudes.

A: He's sexual, or was. But not in an obvious way. He needed quite a bit of stimulation ... I think they came up with that nickname because gossips love things that rhyme. Brief, clever, witty, catchy. 'Sexy Rexy'. (Laughs.) If nothing else, it's catchy.

Q: During the 1960s, he was for a while a top star, but –

A: He never caught on in the States, really. No. Too foreign. Marvellous voice, but not handsome. Cold, overbearing, foppish. You know, when he played Henry Higgins, 'a confirmed old bachelor', he did deserve that award [Oscar], but he came off like somebody's maiden uncle! (Laughs.)

What *made* him, originally, was starring in gossip. Wives, lovers, the Carole Landis suicide ... He genuinely hated all that scandalous publicity. On the other hand, he was so privately grateful to finally become a star. Because before [the play] *My Fair Lady*, he was just about washed up. Then came *Cleopatra*, and how Rex despised Liz and Dick for getting all that publicity! Publicity hogs, he called them, and he used to envy Burton's ability to charm people without even opening his mouth.

Q: What do you think of Lilli Palmer, whom I've always liked?

A:... Chic. Stylish. Plenty of presence on the screen. However, except for Dietrich, Americans have never liked Teutonic females on the silver screen.

Q: Can you credit what I once read, about Harrison sending back the wine in his own house, because it wasn't good enough?

A: (Nods vehemently) He cannot be pleased. Servants

have got slapped with his tongue or hand. Eventually, his servants and wives leave him. Rex is one of those what thinks living well is the best revenge. It may be, but the revenge is taken out on his nearest and his dearest.

Q: Do you think actors should never marry each other?

A: If one is a star, the other gets hell. If both are struggling, they've got each other for moral support. It's the disparity that wounds. More so yet when the star is a born sadist.

Q: You and he fell in love doing a play. By the time you did a film together [*A Flea in Her Ear*], you'd fallen out of love. Was it hard co-starring?

A: Forget the equity, love! He was the star, and I happened to be in it. (Laughs) Rex was nicer to his leading ladies than his wives. They got the pleasant public face. The wives get the cold reality. If we hadn't been shackled together, he'd have flirted with me on the set, just for appearances, for his credentials – those get more important as a man gets older. Rex was always afraid of being past it.

Q: Somewhere I read that Rachel Roberts has, or can have, 'a foul Welsh temper'. True or false?

A: I have a Welsh temperament. What is a Welsh temper?

Q: I suppose something like the so-called Irish temper.

A: And by whose definition? The English! The unruly, fighting Scots. The fighting Irish. The fighting Welsh. Yet who is it fought us all, and kept on fighting, so as to maintain her military might? The English. I rest my case.

Now, this is a fabulous quote, and presumably true. It was when Gandhi – the Mahatma – visited England. In 1930. Some very supercilious English journalist asked him, 'What do you think of modern civilization?' Mr Gandhi answered, 'I think it would be a very good idea.'

Q: In a British film I was recently watching, one character says, 'Black men begin at Calais!'

A: Yeah, or even Swansea …

Q: Can you name some of the British actresses who may have influenced you or whom you particularly liked?

A: (Eyes open very wide) What a large question! (Long

pause.) I remember enjoying seeing actresses like Phyllis Calvert – don't ask me what in ... Margaret Lockwood ... Patricia Roc, Anne Crawford ... Those ladies made wonderful things that I doubt received very good notices, but they gave real pleasure. Of course I also admired the obvious theatrical legends, including Edith Evans – good Welsh name! I admire any actress who remains an actress, does her best with what she's offered. Don't have much regard for the ones that retire at forty or when their beauty fades; that's not acting, that's modelling!

Q: Margaret Lockwood was *The Wicked Lady*. Why do you think the American version required her to cover up her cleavage?

A: Hypocrisy! Yanks love tits as much as anyone. In fact, now they've veered to the other extreme, and they shove tits in your face, at the cinema! They're the ones that came up with Marilyn, and Jayne Mansfield and the rest ... Americans are always trying to over-protect their children, meanwhile depriving adults of healthy adult entertainment, and yet the fact is that American kids grow up as lusty and as mixed a bag as anyone else's children. I think America's a very juvenile-oriented society – in comparison with Europe, at any rate.

Q: It seems to me that American actors love to talk about acting, while the Brits just act. Do you agree?

A: On the whole ... I usually don't have to tell myself, What shall I think of during the death scene to make me cry? It can be as simple as one's fear of death – if one fears it (laughs softly). A certain gesture may bring back strong memory or emotion.

Q: Or a taste or smell may trigger it, as Proust noted.

A: True ... There's a comment from [Ralph Waldo] Emerson that I love. He said, 'That which lies behind us and that which lies before us are tiny matters compared to that which lies within us.'

Q: Within each of us is the universe ...

A: A profound and Eastern philosophy. But universal. As an actor, Emerson's comment signifies living in the moment.

Q: As Stanislavsky taught.

A: Again, it's better to do than simply to talk. Or to watch movies as ... as homework. I used to try to watch old movies, to learn from them. (Shrugs) I'm more of a fan than a student. I only learned from bad movies – how *not* to act, not to indicate or posture. But I still love the golden oldies. (Sighs) I can remember when the only special effects in movies were talent!

Q: Shakespeare said all the world's a stage ...

A: Wasn't the first one to say so, I'm sure. It's true, love. Whoever came up with Honesty Is the Best Policy never had to fake an orgasm. Knew nothing about manners, because if you think about it, all etiquette is socially sanctioned hypocrisy. Like saying somebody looks good when she doesn't, that something tastes good when it doesn't, or you're glad to see somebody and must lunch with him soon, even though he's a bloody bore!

Q: You have a unique slant on things.

A: It comes from all that time sitting around on sets. Gives one time to think! Thinking can be detrimental to one's optimism, but there you are ... It's not that one chooses to be discouraging, but the older one gets, the more disappointed. In life, definitely in people. One doesn't choose to be grim, one just reacts to what is out there. Betrayal is par for the course – in any business or human endeavour, certainly in this fucking business!

Q: No business like show business?

A: (Laughs) To enjoy it, it takes a masochist or a sadist. Nothing in between.

Q: Do you think if you'd started earlier, you might have been – as one critic opined – a British Bette Davis?

A: I never heard that! (delighted) But no ... (sadly) Not in Britain. Until the day of the tart or the day of the average plain housewife, it was the time of the English rose. Period. The Brits liked Bette Davis because she was good – good at being bad! Just as important, she sounded like one of us, yet she came from the States. I could really envy her career. Except, what's the point? I've got enough miseries (smiles).

Q: Do you think people in the business are intimidated by you because of your many aggressive roles?

A: (Nods) That is why, theoretically, it's important to carefully select one's roles. It's not simply the public that believes actors are who they portray. However, in reality, one can only pick or choose from the deck which is offered one, past thirty or forty.

Q: Why do so many actors drink?

A: To excess, you mean (smirking).

Q: Right. And do actors drink more than non-actors?

A: (Groans) When a civilian over-imbibes, he doesn't land on the front page, next day ... Actors have more cause to drink. A mill worker, say. His job is routinely awful. But people can become accustomed to anything. They inure themselves. Actors have no routine. It's a very manic-depressive life. It's glory or it's misery. When you're given a high-paying, exciting job, all is bliss. The bliss may last a few weeks or months, depending.

Then when the job's over, the true misery is the inactivity and the wondering – being alone, unpaid, unwanted, not even sure you'll ever work again. Wondering – am I too old? Too ugly? Has my reputation suffered? Does someone have it in for me? Have I repeated myself into professional oblivion? It's agony.

It's not so difficult to lay off the booze while inside that world of make-believe, that world of playing somebody entirely else and having a character's temporary, cathartic problems. Who thinks of booze at times like that? It's when it's over that booze enters your mind. (Shrugs.) Simply because reality just doesn't measure up.

Q: It's a bit like the saying that when one's busy, one doesn't think as often about food.

A: It is true that people with too much leisure tend to get heavier. Again, food is simply a substitute, a temporary putting aside of drab reality.

Q: Are you quite vain about your looks, which you've kept?

A: You're so sweet! Yes (shyly). I have to be vain, professionally, but I am psychologically, as well.

Q: Do you think it's always a mistake – personally and
professionally – for a talented or idiosyncratic actress like Elsa
Lanchester to marry a man who is a bigger talent and a bigger
star, as with Charles Laughton?

A: ... Or like Rachel Roberts and whatsisname?

Q: Either or both, yes.

A: (Laughs) I'm glad I've made you a little uncomfortable,
because your question made *me* a little uncomfortable! Rex
was by all means a bigger star than me, though not a bigger
talent ... It is a mistake, professionally. Not socially. Not
while it lasts. Everyone has her own hell, but being a star's
wife is at least a gold-plated hell! Professionally ... well, look
at Richard Burton. The first thing any reporter wants to know
from him is, Is he in or out with Liz? It's best not to be placed
in a situation of comparisons. And hindsight is better than ...
whatever it is.

Q: After you, Harrison stopped marrying actresses –

A: Well, why marry an actress when you can marry the
daughter of a baron [Elizabeth Harris]? That's not even
competition!

Q: And you stopped marrying actors ...

A: Or anyone else, in fact. I doubt I would marry again. I
know I would not marry an actor again. Not unless he's rich,
very old and fatally ill. If you know anyone meeting that
description, do send him round! (Laughs.)

Q: Do you have any acting goals left?

A: Well, as I'm not yet eighty, I would say I do ... Success!

Q: How do you define success?

A: On the everyday level, it's having a reason to get out of
bed in the morning – or early afternoon (smiles). Enjoying
each day, at least some part of it. As an actress, success is being
rich, famous and desired – nothing less.

Foul Play did not yield plum parts for Rachel Roberts, whose
reputation as a top-calibre but older and foreign actress kept

Hollywood from casting her in the small but profitable roles she'd likely have accepted. Those who did seek her out were increasingly wary of her alcoholism and dependence on pills. Though advised against it, she did a play titled *The Sorrows of Gin* and signed on for B-films such as *When a Stranger Calls* and *Charlie Chan and the Curse of the Dragon Queen* (Angie Dickinson played the second title role, with Roberts as Mrs Dangers in the 1980 disaster).

Her final role was even smaller than usual, but in a quality offering, *The Wall*, a 1981 CBS telefilm. It was set in Treblinka, the concentration camp in which thousands from the Warsaw ghetto were incinerated under the Nazis. The project was shot in Poland, with Auschwitz substituting for Treblinka. Rachel was cast as the landlady of Tom Conti, a member of the Polish underground.

Stopping off in London to see Lindsay Anderson, Rachel collapsed and was taken to the Royal Free Hospital in Hampstead. Her addictions were catching up with her, as was her obsession with Rex Harrison and the (very remote) possibility of re-marrying him (as Richard Burton had Elizabeth Taylor; Rachel had become close to Taylor while their husbands had co-starred as gay lovers in *Staircase*, 1969). An anonymous associate reveals:

'At almost the end of her life, Ray knew she was hopelessly alcoholic. She believed only Rex could save her. She felt he was turning back the clock by doing a revival tour of *My Fair Lady*, and that her career and happiness could be revived by Rex taking her back ... She had already tried to take her own life, and failed, usually a hint that one wants to live.

'When she realized Rex would never take her back, couldn't take her back, she contemplated a change of career. Something as drastic and tragic as giving up acting to become a secretary at an agency,' probably because her Welsh friend Sybil Christopher (whom Burton had divorced to marry Taylor the first time) was working at the ICM talent agency in Hollywood. 'But Ray knew she could never stand something so anonymous, not to mention demanding. It was just a matter of time and means until her constant talk of death took a lethal form ...'

The time was 26 November 1980. The means were pills and poison. This time, Rachel planned it so nothing could go wrong, even remembering to eat a crumpet, or 'English muffin', so she wouldn't vomit up the pills. Then she took poison, as an added precaution. Insiders said she planned the event to coincide with the Los Angeles opening of Rex Harrisons's *My Fair Lady* tour, so as to steal his headlines and dampen the publicity for the seventy-two-year-old's triumphant return to Hollywood.

Lilli Palmer, who had been married to Harrison when Carole Landis committed suicide over him, explained, 'Rachel probably wanted to prove she could still compete with Rex ... But I believe the Central American gardener came a day later than intended, and so she didn't make the headlines on the day she wanted. The local coroner didn't disclose or know that it was a suicide until days later ... In a way, it was a Britannic version of *A Star Is Born*, only much more complex.'

Most of the stars and members of the Hollywood British colony expressed surprise and loss at Rachel Roberts's passing. Some were sad but not at all surprised. Her friend Sybil Christopher declared, 'When she died, I felt she had got what she wanted at last – peace. Every time I hear John Lennon's song "Woman", I am weeping for *her*.'

9

Dame Flora Robson

*Dame Flora Robson retired to Brighton, where she died in
1984. 'I always loved sunshine and the seashore. By rights,
I should have long since transplanted myself to California.'
In 1980 we took a clotted-cream tea and had a leisurely
interview in the small restaurant of the Royal Pavilion at
Brighton. Dame Flora enjoyed talking about her adopted
home-town, where she did regular charitable work and
kept abreast of local theatre. 'I always find things are
happier by the sea.'*

'I suppose I'm best remembered for my Elizabeth I.
Even Americans are familiar with *Fire Over England*. I
felt very much at home as the queen. The physical
similarity wasn't astonishing to me. Most of my childhood,
I'd identified with the Virgin Queen and dreamed of
emulating her in one way or another. When I donned her
gowns and wigs for the part, it somehow seemed
pre-ordained, almost a reincarnation experience.'

Many critics hold that Robson's Elizabeth was truer to life
than, and outshone the interpretations of, among others,
Bette Davis, Florence Eldridge and Glenda Jackson. 'I envy
Miss Davis. Like me, she played Elizabeth when young. But

she got to play her again in middle age in yet another film ...
I think Miss Jackson's performances [for British TV] were
stunning, and were emotionally right on the mark.'

It was chiefly because of the 1936 film success *Fire Over
England* that Robson, who had a four-year contract with
British film producer Alexander Korda, went to Hollywood.
She worked there from 1939-42:

'They wanted to keep me busy, the notion being that
imported English actors lent tone to Hollywood productions, if not box office allure ... I had glamorous actors to
support – Errol Flynn, Gary Cooper, Olivier of course, and
Niven, and lovely Merle Oberon in *Wuthering Heights*
[1939].'

Of her role as Ingrid Bergman's mulatto retainer in
Saratoga Trunk (1942), she said, 'To my face, I was
complimented on my versatile plainness! An executive or
in-law, who said that with my face I could play any
nationality. I did, for I had the generous lips – now thinner
with age – to play a mulatto, and much later I was requested
to be a Chinese empress,' in *55 Days at Peking* (1962),
'which I felt was only logical!'

At best, Dame Flora's face was handsome, and in repose
blank. Her voice could fill with menace or warmth, and her
characters were never predictable. She was too indeciphera-
ble to become stereotyped, even on screen, and shuttled
between women of quality and working-class figures,
benefactresses and villains. What she did not often do was
comedy. She explained, 'My personal inclination is towards
a character who feels more profoundly than she at first lets
on ...' Critic Ronald Barker put it this way in 1955: 'Flora
Robson, a superb emotional actress, has not the ease
required for light comedy or farce. She makes us feel so
deeply that we are afraid to laugh.'

Film critic Wyatt Cooper opined, 'Robson is a star on the
stage because her feeling shines through, whatever the role.
On the screen, her phlegmatic nature and equine looks can
overwhelm a role if it's not sufficiently strong.'

While deftly buttering a scone, Dame Flora told me, 'I fell in love with acting as a little girl. Thank goodness! By the time I was attempting to become an actress, it was too late to ask myself if my face would be a liability.'

She was born Flora McKenzie Robson in South Shields, County Durham, in 1902. Her father, a marine engineer, took pride in her fine voice and encouraged her to recite. At six, Flora's father took her to see the play *Faust* in London (where they had moved), 'and I chose acting, although it might be more romantic to say that it chose me'. In time, she enrolled at RADA (Royal Academy of Dramatic Art) and in 1921 graduated with a bronze medal. That year marked her professional début in *Will Shakespeare*, a one-line role as the ghost of Queen Margaret.

She joined Ben Greet's Pastoral Players in 1922, acting in rep in twenty plays, al fresco. A rare grin crossed Dame Flora's face as she recalled, 'We did those plays in the open air, a novel concept, then. In one interview [for an Australian paper], I used the phrase "al fresco", and the young man asked, "Al who?" It was wicked of me, but I couldn't help responding, "Al Fresco – a first cousin to Art Deco." He took it very well. Most Aussies have a reliable sense of humour.'

In 1923 Flora joined the company at the Oxford Playhouse for two seasons. One of her colleagues was Tyrone Guthrie, who would become closely involved with her professional life. After a brief turn on stage in London in 1924, the offers suddenly dried up, and Flora went back to her parents, by then living in Welwyn Garden City. At a Shredded Wheat factory she took employment as an assistant in public relations and personnel. 'I was there four years ... Not as bad as it sounds, because the firm had an amateur theatre group, and I got to direct it.'

In 1929, with Guthrie as her go-between, she joined the Cambridge Festival Theatre. Her year and a half there included *Six Characters in Search of an Author*. In 1931 she transferred to London, where she played the young wife (eventually portrayed on screen by Sophia Loren!) in O'Neill's *Desire Under the Elms*. Frequently cast against type, she was also Herodias in *Salomé* and an alcoholic harlot in *The Anatomist*. 'I suppose I was too naïve to question whether I could portray such characters.'

Critic St John Ervine rhapsodized, 'Here is an actress. If you are not moved by this girl's performance, then you are immovable and have no right to be on this earth.'

'I got to play Bianca in *Othello*, and did J.B. Priestley's maiden play, *Dangerous Corner*.' Co-star Ralph Richardson (in Maugham's *For Services Rendered*) declared, 'Flora is a born actress. She can act anything, is believable always – because she does not act, she *is*.'

Charles Laughton, head of the Old Vic-Sadler's Wells company, invited Robson to be part of their 1933-4 season. 'It was bliss being directed by Tyrone Guthrie again. In his or her career, a typical actor finds one or two directors who stand head and shoulders above the rest. Mine was Guthrie.' Lady Macbeth was her stand-out role that season, but she also excelled in *The Cherry Orchard*, *Henry VIII* (as Katharine of Aragon), *Measure for Measure*, *The Importance of Being Earnest* (as Gwendolyn), *Love For Love* and *The Tempest*.

Flora Robson's acclaim reached the ear and eye of Sir Alexander Korda, who signed her for films. 'I was in seventh heaven at the prospect!' she reminisced. 'From a mercenary point of view, the money meant I should never have to return to a non-acting job. Yet I was equally intent upon working regularly and in better roles than I'd already had in the cinema.'

Her screen bow had been *Gentleman of Paris* (1931). In 1933 she was the old empress in the Elisabeth Bergner vehicle *Catherine the Great*, then ruled the screen in Korda's *Fire Over England*, co-starring Laurence Olivier and Vivien Leigh. 'Ordinarily, I would have been hesitant about sharing film scenes with Vivien, who was so ethereally attractive. But I was Elizabeth ...'

The following year she worked in the aborted and now legendary *I, Claudius* starring Charles Laughton and directed by Joseph Von Sternberg. 'It was ill-fated,' she wistfully remembered. 'Merle Oberon's [car] accident was the last straw. Had it been completed, it would have been visually and morally lavish ... I was the old poisoner, Livia. She was a schemer on an atrocious scale, Rome's first empress – married to Augustus – and she killed off all the competition to place her own son on the throne.'

How did Dame Flora like playing bad women?

'I prefer it,' she smiled. 'More meat.'

After signing with Korda, Robson did not immediately begin filming. 'He gave me a script to read, while they prepared something for me. He got James Bridie to write *Mary Read* for me. It was about the famous – well, famous *here* – lady pirate. She was an actual swashbuckling pirate who got away with it by dressing in men's clothes; her friend Anne Bonny did the same thing! It was a somewhat avant-garde play, but it went on at the end of 1934 at His Majesty's Theatre.'

Flora's mentor Tyrone Guthrie was adamantly opposed to her wearing male garments on the stage. 'He had my best interests at heart, even if he was rather hidebound in some of his ideas. We didn't always agree on the plays I chose. But when it's your name up in lights, you must choose, and I find it best to go by instinct. I couldn't go by commercial considerations alone, even if they were sound – and they aren't, for one cannot second-guess the public, as I well realize.'

In 1935 she went from *Mary Read* to *Mary Tudor*, again in the title role. Two years later she was the waterfront prostitute *Anna Christie*, which role had launched Garbo's talkie screen career.

Said Dame Flora: 'Restrospect fascinates me. During the doing of something, we have a perspective. Or rather, none, for we're caught up in the project. Years and years later, one wonders that one did the project at all. What dawned on me long after the fact, and some ways impressed or surprised me, was the number of ladies of ill-repute in my repertoire!

'My emoting was apparently a first-rate catharsis. I must have chosen a quantity of my characters on the basis of their alien-ness to my own emotional life ...'

In 1939, Flora Robson went to Hollywood. 'Whatever I expected, I didn't find. The citizenry was attractive, but I found little depth there ... With the situation in Europe, I was homesick, and I missed the theatre.' In 1940 she made her Broadway bow in *Ladies in Retirement*. While in America, Robson kept busy on stage. In 1941 in New York she was the Duchess of Marlborough in *Anne of England*, and in 1942 toured summer theatres as *Elizabeth the Queen*, which was 'how they preferred to see me.

'In Los Angeles, time and again I was mistaken for an actress named Anne Revere, whom I was said to resemble. People were happier when I donned my red wig, pearls and gowns as the Virgin Queen, although once I was mistaken for Bette Davis, whom I do not resemble at all!'

In 1943 Robson was at the Belasco Theatre in LA, doing Grand Guignol plays. Next year, she was back in England for the reopening of the Lyric, Hammersmith, as Thérèse Raquin in *Guilty*, from Emile Zola's novel.

Audrey Williamson wrote, 'This was emotional acting of rare power in which face, voice and gesture mirrored the sickening agony and fear of a character not strong enough to face the consequences of murder. Obliged to play against her physical type, she nevertheless painted a nervously vital portrait of the sensuous and passion-fevered Thérèse.'

Robson took time out to portray Cleopatra's aggressively faithful servant Ftatateeta in Shaw's *Caesar and Cleopatra* (1945). The Vivien Leigh/Claude Rains-starrer was Britain's most expensive film to date, and Flora was thrilled to meet Shaw on the set. 'He was an enchanting white pixie, ageless, like a child. Not the stuffy philosopher or faddist pictured by the press. A principled but gentle man.'

The same year, she undertook a tour of the provinces,

bringing culture to 'drab provincial centres ... Some actresses prefer to stay at home rather than tour. Not I. If I had wanted to come home every evening – or morning – I would have stayed with cereal. Touring provided new audiences, new surroundings and fresh emotional ammunition for a long run.'

In 1948 she played in Shaw's *Captain Brassbound's Conversion*, and had a meaty, villainous role in the haunting film *Saraband For Dead Lovers* (*Saraband* in the US). 'During and after my little Hollywood sojourn, my screen roles were not of a foreground prominence ... In this film, I got to vamp and be hateful and to scheme, while presenting history. A terrible fragment of history, about the machinations leading to our first German king [George I]. Joan Greenwood was the heroine, so beautiful and so very much the victim.

'Watching it later, I loathed my character and felt for poor Joan. It was a tragic story; she was utterly sacrificed to Hanoverian lust for power ... An example of the vast power of celluloid to move and inform us – too often wasted.'

Not herself a mother, Flora Robson had one of her greatest stage triumphs as a disturbed mother who becomes a shoplifter in *Black Chiffon* in 1949. 'You needn't be it to play it. As far as I'm concerned, one of the most touching and real screen renditions of mother-love was Garbo's in *Anna Karenina*. She didn't marry or have offspring, either.'

One critic said of *Black Chiffon*'s star: '[She] is true and unexaggerated, as she always is in the presentation of emotional distress.' Another: 'Miss Robson is magnificent in this part. Is there any other actress playing today who can suggest so much feeling with so little fuss?' In late 1950 she took the play to Broadway.

A succession of stage roles ensued, including Miss Giddens in *The Innocents* in 1952. 'It was a governess role, and by and large those are unsatisfying to an actor. Audiences lap them up, if the children are precious and the other ingredients suitable. Look at Julie Andrews's governesses (in *Mary Poppins* and *The Sound of Music*) ... But I accepted the role because Henry James had invested it with an ambiguity that also makes the children intriguing and the audience involved.'

Estelle Winwood, who had co-starred with her in *Ladies in Retirement*, offered, 'Flora is a secret psychologist. She does not hold with the tomfoolery which they call method acting, but she's a great one for unearthing a character's motivation and her deepest, darkest secrets!'

Thus, Flora's comedies were few and generally unsuccessful. She flourished in the 1950s in heavy roles: Mrs Alving in *Ghosts* and Miss Tina in *The Aspern Papers* with Michael Redgrave, who dubbed her 'the actress who made worry into an art form'. As Miss Tina, she earned the *Evening Standard* Award for Best Actress in 1960. Peter Roberts said, 'A performance that must surely rank as the greatest in her career.

'Watch her, for instance, in the second act when she appears in an unfamiliar best dress with an unfamiliar coiffure. She is in a state of agitated expectancy yet has spoken no line that hints of a new dress, coiffure or agitation. But she conveys all these things, and much more, in a few seconds.'

In 1960 she became Dame Flora Robson and took *The Aspern Papers* on tour to South Africa. The next year, she was Miss Moffatt in *The Corn Is Green*, playing it in South Africa and at the Flora Robson Playhouse in Newcastle-upon-Tyne. 'I always feel that one is most fully and expectantly alive when one is travelling.' Her 1962 film *55 Days at Peking* took her to Spain, which doubled as Chinese background for stars Charlton Heston, Ava Gardner and David Niven.

'Bobby Helpmann was there to help me with my morale. Unlike the stage, a movie set or location does not abound in camaraderie. It's a most undemocratic business. Each of the stars had a little clique and seemed to vie with each other for

Flora Robson as Elizabeth I in *Fire Over England*, 1936.

Dame Flora in *Seven Women*, 1965. (*Doug McClelland*)

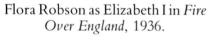

Dame Flora and Rod Taylor in *Young Cassidy*, 1964. (*Doug McClelland*)

Margaret Rutherford as Agatha Christie's Miss Marple.

Dame Margaret in her Oscar-winning role in *The VIPs*, 1963, with Martin Miller and Richard Wattis. (*Doug McClelland*)

inaccessibility ... David was as always a gentleman, and we did chat between takes, but he too had "gone Hollywood", and was surrounded by minions. I'm sure that if I had fun or laughed at all, it was due to Bobby's good graces. Besides which, playing an empress the age of a minor pyramid isn't very comfortable, thanks to the slanted eyes, headdress, rigid posture, and so on. I told Bobby that he had it very easy, in comparison – he played a eunuch!

'When I viewed the finished product, I was appalled. Ostensibly it was about the Boxer Rebellion. If you read your history, you know that some 20 million Chinese died during that legitimate rebellion against European colonialism and greed. It was a very biased film!'

With age, Dame Flora's screen characters were increasingly villainous or accursed, or both. In *Murder at the Gallop* (1963) she was the surprise murderer who tries to do in Jane Marple with a lethal hatpin. There was criticism that her character's guilt was unfairly concealed till the last via another actress's voiceover during a crucial will-reading scene in which Robson is heavily veiled while impersonating another woman. 'It was quite jolly, working with Margaret [Rutherford] and Robert [Morley]. Their company, the camaraderie ...

'I got to play an absolute mouse most of the time. She was even supposedly afraid of Miss Marple, suspecting *her* of murder. Then, once I showed my true face, the woman's greed spewed forth, for she had repeatedly killed for the sake of a valuable painting ... Oddly satisfying film, that one.'

In 1964 Dame Flora attended the reception given by the Queen to commemorate 400 years since Shakespeare's birth. 'It was a magnificent gathering of the sorority. And the fraternity,' she added. The same year, after heavy emoting in Ibsen, she was Miss Prism in *The Importance of Being Earnest* at her namesake theatre in Newcastle, later returning to form as Hecuba in *The Trojan Women*, then touring in a variety of vehicles.

Did such a busy and peripatetic schedule leave her room for a private life?

'Oh, yes. Yes, it did.' But she noted, a mite severely – and why not? Brighton isn't Hollywood – 'Any actor who manages to create audience interest has to reach an important decision, and early on. That is, to have either a private life or, at most, a semi-private one. If you talk about it in public, for publication, it's no longer a private life. Mine *is.*'

I asked, towards the end of our tea-laced session, 'Do you have any personal regrets stemming from your career?'

She shook her head vehemently, surprised. 'Oh, no! In every way, my career has enriched my life ... Thanks to success in my chosen career, I've been able with few and minor exceptions to live the life I wanted.'

In 1965 Dame Flora was directed by John Ford in *Seven Women*. Its female cast included Anne Bancroft, Margaret Leighton and Sue Lyon. 'Not an easy location, and it was a grim film, but it was made rather remarkable by Mr Ford. He did have one habit that I found disconcerting, though. He used to carry about a handkerchief, originally white but by then probably the filthiest-looking piece of cloth you ever laid eyes on.

'He would mop his brow with it, and occasionally the brows of particular members of the cast,' she shudder-laughed. 'Other than that, he was a likeable tyrant, I suppose because in his decline. But after all our work, and despite his ferociously elevated status, the picture *fell*. Nobody saw it. I'm not sure if it isn't Mr Ford's least seen of all his films.'

She explained, 'After being under contract to Mr Korda and finding it wasn't the hoped-for heaven, I tried Hollywood. It was worse ... The further I went in films, the more disappointments, until I steeled myself not to expect much from film. It's just a diversion, really. I always prefer the stage.'

Through the mid-1960s, Dame Flora continued touring, but by the decade's end was sticking to London and its environs. In 1964 she played Lady Bracknell in *The Importance of Being*

Earnest, and four years later did Miss Prism in the same comedy classic. 'The two are polar opposites, and I'd always wanted to try them both on. One doesn't look for hidden meaning in Oscar Wilde – his meaning is on the glittering surface.

'But as someone who isn't always at home in comedy, I can appreciate that Wilde wrote his characters so they would be actor-proof. The laughs come, regardless.'

Helen Dawson felt, 'Flora Robson almost makes it Miss Prism's play – stumbling with embarrassed gestures, grabbing back words she accidentally let out, greeting her gentleman friend's every phrase as though it were a revelation. Her joy in the last act at retrieving her handbag is a highpoint of stage ecstasy.'

The same critic voiced dismay when Robson acted in Jean Anouilh's *Ring Round the Moon*: 'Flora Robson seemed a little unsure of how frivolous she was allowed to be as the Mother with an eye to the main chance.'

In 1969 Dame Flora was on more familiar ground as Agatha Payne in *The Old Ladies*. Said Hugh Leonard, '[She] played the villainous Mrs Payne with a gleeful sense of black humour. Self-preservation was the keynote, whether Dame Flora was popping a slice of cake into her reticule or negotiating the stairs with the concentration of a bomb-disposal expert.'

In 1970 she was Elizabeth once more, in *Elizabeth Tudor* at the Edinburgh Festival. Four years later, she made her last stage appearance at the Brighton Festival, narrating *Peter and the Wolf*. By then she had retired to Brighton, where her hobbies included charity, making tapestry and socializing. Also watching horror movies on TV: 'I even watch mine, sometimes. A few hold up, such as *Eye of the Devil*,' a 1966 entry with Deborah Kerr and David Niven. 'I think psychology is the key to horror, not bad makeup or ludicrous monsters. I indict my own judgment when I admit that I appeared in something like *The Beast in the Cellar* (1970). The shooting wasn't bad, but the result was.

'There's so much they can put into a film that isn't in the script, such as bad special effects and monsters that are laughable or disgusting, not terrifying. There's simply too much bad taste in the genre now. Too obvious ... But I suppose they will always think of me in connection with that genre of film. At least here in England.'

Indeed, Dame Flora's last picture was the English-made Olympian epic *Clash of the Titans* (1981), with an all-star cast (Olivier, Claire Bloom, Maggie Smith, Ursula Andress, Harry Hamlin). The veteran actress was wasted as one of three blind witches, in a rather brief and needlessly grotesque scene. In the 1970s, she had done some television, participating in small-screen adaptations such as *A Tale of Two Cities*, *Les Misérables*, *Heidi* and *The Canterville Ghost*.

'The racing tempo of television isn't to my ideal taste,' she reasoned, 'but what would older actors do without television? The stage is so demanding of our energy and memory, and there comes a time ... while film is a medium in which stage actors play character parts, often minuscule although more interesting than the leading characters.

'Television does the sort of spectacle or classic which films used to do. It offers frequent employment if one isn't too exacting. On the set, one meets other older actors, and we commiserate with our eyes ...'

Basil Dearden, who directed her *Saraband For Dead Lovers*, believed, 'Flora has the range of any one of the best movie actresses. Only light comedy escaped her. Had she started sooner in Hollywood and been viewed as one of their own, she might have gone far. Like [Bette] Davis, she could convincingly portray a kindly soul or a venomous shrew.

'Of course, two things worked against her on screen. Her face could not suggest beauty, as many non-beauties were able to do ... and the stolid quality which she camouflaged on stage through histrionics and disciplined craft.'

Dame Flora admitted, 'I do become discouraged when I rediscover that talent isn't as essential as we like to think. It's one of the reasons I seldom returned to Hollywood – besides that, I wasn't often asked.'

One such discovery occurred during Robson's Hollywood 'sojourn' while enacting housekeeper Nelly Dean in *Wuthering Heights*. 'The part was negligible, but the other factors were not. I sailed with high hopes which were dashed almost upon my arrival in the States ... In New York, an Englishman telephoned to my hotel and brusquely informed me that photographers would shortly arrive, for publicity's sake. They took a mass of photos, more than any number of publications could possibly use, and next day sent me a huge bill! It was obviously a racket.

'I called Hollywood for help or advice, and was instead ordered to pay up immediately, or else I might be sued and create bad publicity for the studio. I did not pay, they did not sue, and I did not trust unquestioningly after that ... Then, in Hollywood, I arrived at the studio only to be greeted by a man with a gun who bellowed at me, 'What do you want?' I said I was there for a hairdressing test, but he didn't believe me, and refused to telephone the individual in charge! It was mortifying. Somehow I shamefacedly made my way to a place designated 'Entrance For Extras', where a young woman finally let me in.

'As you know, Larry Olivier was in the film, and I was somewhat – I say *somewhat* – mollified when he said he'd received the exact same treatment upon trying to enter the studio! It transpired that the reason was the American mistrust of anybody who tries to enter a building on foot. Stars and featured players were supposed to arrive by car ...

'My next jolt was when I found my salary would not enable me to live in a hotel. I had to find an apartment for the duration, and Hollywood landlords had the appalling habit of extracting two months' rent upfront. This, due to the frequency of would-be actors departing without paying their rent after discovering that movie roles didn't grow on orange trees! Very gruff men, those landlords, and they didn't realize that in my own country I was not an unknown, nor a potential ... "deadbeat".'

On the positive side, director William Wyler invited Flora to attend script conferences with scenarist John Huston. 'Mr Wyler knew that the novel was a classic in my country, and asked me to speak up if anything sounded overly American. And Mr Huston had lived for a time in England.'

Wyler was very pleased with Flora's performance, though her role had been shortened in order to augment that of young Merle Oberon. He decided to use the older actress's voice as narration, and even let her write her own script. 'I was ecstatic. I'd risen through merit. I was terribly eager to please … But then I discovered that after our film was completed, it was to be "tested" by an audience of adolescents – "teenagers".

'Why? I asked. They said that if the room full of children happened to laugh or even giggle during a scene when it wasn't appropriate, then that scene would be excised! Why should *they* decide? I asked. I was told in all seriousness that the average age of a cinema patron in the States was sixteen … Which is why I'm amused when I hear people complain that nowadays the youth market has taken over motion pictures.'

I asked Flora Robson what was her worst experience as an actress? 'Theatre or film?' she asked. Either, I said.

'Nothing horribly traumatic on the stage,' she smiled. 'It's a homely, happier place … The ups and downs of film are much more intense, and can take place within minutes of each other. In the early days, I would get nervous on film sets. I became exceedingly nervous with *Catherine the Great* [1933]. It was a tense place. Our version would compete with a Hollywood version made by Mr Von Sternberg, starring Miss Dietrich. Our director was Paul Czinner, now perhaps forgotten, but then characterized as a great artist and a near-genius.

'The star was Elisabeth Bergner, and Mr Czinner knew how to manage her generous temperament. In the theatre, I was usually among friends; at Elstree [studios] I was a stranger, the outsider. The leading man was Douglas

Fairbanks Jr. He seemed very much a star, and obviously had his father as an example. But he could be kind. I was dressed in a mountain of royal Russian finery, and became rather tongue-tied. I was standing next to Mr Fairbanks, who was the soul of nonchalance.

'He turned towards me, looked me up and down, smiled and said, "I just can't believe you're real. I keep thinking if I lift you up by the neck, there'll be a telephone underneath you!" We both laughed, and I felt better at once.'

A disappointment was in store when Flora, reading up on the real Great Kate, saw that the script had been tailored to Bergner (Czinner's wife), not to historical veracity. 'As an example, our film pretended that Catherine was faithful to one man, only feigning multiple lovers in order to win her husband's affections! The facts of her labyrinthine lusts were totally ignored! My character was also enamoured of men, although not to Catherine's exorbitant degree. This was my first major film, and I found the so-called love scenes – though entirely chaste by current standards – to be my most difficult ones.'

She continued, 'Anyway, film represented a small fraction of my career. It takes so little time, but yields so much publicity and recognition. Nor were those two commodities which I deliberately sought. I sincerely like people and am a good talker, but being adulated on the street does make me uncomfortable. I never try to make myself conspicuous in public.

'One of my best experiences in the theatre was when John Van Druten, a superlative playwright and gentleman, wrote a play for me. It was called *The Damask Cheek*. Mr Van Druten was the type of person who gifted one with a spiritual energy, and a gladness. He was a Hindu and an intellectual, so very kindly and helpful – treating all people alike, whether stars, ordinary actors or non-actors.

'Had he been based in England, I'm sure we would have become good friends and colleagues. It's a pity much of his work is overlooked now, for he wrote witty, outstanding plays and film scripts. He was immensely successful, but it never went to his head, and he wrote a play for *me* when he could have written a play or film for Hollywood's foremost actresses!'

Another special memory was reserved for Charles Laughton. 'He gave me a lot of wonderful advice. He would confide how before his tremendous stardom, his one great regret was being physically unattractive. But in Hollywood he realized that his unique face would stand him in good stead as an actor, as someone who would be remembered long after the pretty young things were forgotten. After achieving stardom, his great regret was having wasted his youth regretting how he looked!

'Besides the work that we shared, he helped give me an outlook on my professional life and my looks. Through him, I came to the conclusion that actors not blessed with beauty are actually happier in their careers, and not because they're unusual. The attractive ones I've worked with typically expect the good life and careers to be handed to them on a plate. They get jaded far too easily. Mr Laugton said he could appreciate his great good fortune every time he looked in the mirror.

'I myself had often wondered if I would be able to earn my keep as an actress. When I worked at the cereal plant, I wondered if I would ever be given the chance to go back to the professional theatre … No matter how far I went, in my modest way, I couldn't help retaining a certain humility and secret joy that I was even in the profession, let alone succeeding nicely!'

She concluded, 'Charles used to say, "Never not dare to hang yourself." It was his motto and his advice to fellow actors. He encouraged my sometimes "offbeat" play choices, for we both felt that routine and repetition are death for an actor.

'Charles said that the plain man or woman isn't threatened by time the way that one with beauty is. It's true – being handsome or beautiful is like being born rich, but growing unavoidably poorer every day of one's life …'

10

Dame Margaret Rutherford

Margaret Rutherford and her husband Stringer Davis
were, in his words, 'very dear friends', and constant
companions. So, when Dame Margaret consented to be
interviewed over tea at the Savoy, she brought along Davis.
I instantly recognized him as Mr Stringer, the mild-
mannered librarian who served as Miss Marple's sidekick
in four Agatha Christie films. The elderly pair were
exceedingly grateful for the tea, and as delightful and gentle
as two people in, or out of, the movies could be.

When Judith Anderson was asked what difference being a Dame had made in her life, she replied, 'I find myself wearing gloves more often.' Margaret Rutherford was created a DBE in 1967, five years before her death at eighty. She'd described the honour as 'such an uplift', but when I inquired how it really affected her life, her owl-like eyes fluttered hesitantly. 'I do have to be careful to dress better in public.' My eyes avoided the tweed jacket, man's watch and no-nonsense shoes. As if reading my thoughts, she snickered, then breathlessly confided, 'Truth to tell, it is very nice. But it doesn't much affect one's life.

Alas, it affects one's career not at all.

'Such an honour may affect how people think of you or treat you. It does not remove a few decades, and time is an actor's greatest enemy ... When I was awarded the Oscar [for *The VIPS*, 1963], *that* made a difference. People on the other side of the pond [Hollywood] who only knew that I could be funny suddenly decided I could act – which was nice.'

The would-be tragedienne's destiny was to be cast as an endearing eccentric in comedy gem after comedy dross, alternately. Invariably, she was as good as or better than her material. Margaret Rutherford always afforded audiences the thrill of recognition – 'I'm everyone's favourite auntie' – and sustained it, whatever the role. She insisted, 'I'm not the women I've played. Most were eternally jolly. *I* do have a darker side ...'

She spoke of her roles and career in the past tense, for her final film was *Arabella*, a 1967 Virna Lisi vehicle. Her penultimate screen role was a dotty dowager confined to bed in Charlie Chaplin's 1966 *A Countess From Hong Kong*: 'He persuaded me to do it via his own modesty. My role was as nothing compared to Marlon Brando's or Sophia Loren's, but Mr Chaplin assured me that my part would be much bigger than his!'

Despite her comedic image, Dame Margaret's 'darker side' commenced shortly after her birth in South London on 11 May 1892. When Peggy, as her family knew her, was three, her mother hanged herself from a tree (Margaret's father had killed his own father). She was sent to live with a maiden aunt who loved the theatre, and at eight the budding thespian made her début in an amateur theatrical as a fairy prince. 'I played a lot of lads, my dear.'

At school, she played Prospero in *The Tempest*. 'I would have been perfectly content to keep doing Shakespeare until I dropped.' Instead, a forceful headmistress persuaded her to take up the piano, for six years. 'I became a music teacher. I didn't love it, but I did it to earn a living and help my adoptive mother.' Aunt Bessie tried to shield Peggy from the facts of her parental tragedies, but once the young woman found out, she suffered from periodic melancholia which eventually led to nervous breakdowns, rest-home visits and, late in life, the fear that she might be succumbing to hereditary insanity.

Aunt Bessie died when Margaret was thirty-three, leaving her a small inheritance which enabled her to abandon teaching and join the Old Vic as a student. Her first speaking part was The Fairy with the Long Nose. She also did the off-stage lines of a mute male angel, played by Edith Evans. One acerbic critic wrote, 'Edith Evans's elocution has greatly improved.' (Rutherford also played Lady Capulet to Evans's Nurse in *Romeo and Juliet*.)

Despite the dissenting notice, 'I did not set the world on fire,' and after nine months, Margaret was dismissed by the queen of the Old Vic, Lilian Baylis: 'Somehow you just do not fit in!' So it was back to teaching, 'for two discouraging years. I was living in Wimbledon, I was by myself, I was teaching piano, and I rather felt life was passing me by. My cruel reality was that I was living in relative poverty and professionally hampered by my lack of a typical actress's fair looks.'

It wasn't until the age of thirty-six that Margaret decided to wear lipstick. 'As far as cosmetics were concerned,' she chuckled, 'I was a complete virgin. In those days, a well-bred young lady wore mascara at the peril of her good reputation.'

In 1931, nearly forty, the sometime actress began to make her mark, in Oxford, as Lady Bracknell – the role later patented by Edith Evans – in Oscar Wilde's *The Importance of Being Earnest*. At forty-one, she made her West End début in *Wild Justice*. Still, the offers did not arrive in quantity:

'If I had been merely ambitious, I would never have become a celebrity or a known actress. I would have long since quit. But I dearly loved my profession and foolishly clung to it. Can there be any doubt that I was a very late bloomer?'

In 1935 Tyrone Guthrie engaged the character actress to play Miss Flower in Robert Morley's first play, *Short Story*. Critic James Agate reported, 'As a ruthless village spinster [she] entrances and convulses the house every moment she is on the stage.' Success, at last!

'When I was young, I would never have imagined myself a part of the cinema,' confessed Dame Margaret, heartily yet elegantly sipping her tea. 'Moving pictures were the domain of what you could accurately describe as the beautiful people.' None the less, in 1936 began a long and successful, if sometimes underrated, movie career. *Dusty Ermine* was unaccountably retitled *Hideout in the Alps* for the American market. The following year, she appeared in *Beauty and the Barge*, explaining, 'I did not play either of the title characters.'

Most of her work at the time was in the theatre – the comic roles which failed to satisfy her. In her heart, Rutherford told the press more than once, she was really Juliet. 'There have been many parts I yearned to play. How I would love to have been a great traditional actress like Bernhardt, Duse or Ellen Terry.' Privately, she admitted that she envied Edith Evans's career; though far from beautiful, Evans was able to enact the dramatic and even sensual roles that always eluded Margaret's grasp.

In old age, the two Dames were on excellent terms, though openly competitive. Early on, the dramatic laurels went to Edith, the comedic ones to Margaret. The two women's good friend and frequent director John Gielgud declared, 'Evans was often pigeon-holed as a domineering matriarch, Rutherford as a slightly less domineering bachelor.' In Gielgud's 1938 play *Spring Meeting*, Margaret's character was called by Ivor Brown 'a fussy, irritable old maid with a great contempt for marriage'.

Gielgud's legendary 1939 production of *The Importance of Being Earnest* pitted Evans's Lady Bracknell against Rutherford's Miss Prism, one of Margaret's most famous and frequently revived roles. 'I liked the fact that Prism is a strong character – an instructress, in fact – with comic nuances. She is not at all clownish. She has fewer lines than Bracknell, but is a formidable presence in her own right.' *The Times* chortled, 'Miss Rutherford's bridling over the restored handbag, as if it were a favourite cat long lost and now astonishingly mewing in her lap, is as restrained and effective a piece of drollery as one could wish for.' Rutherford's Prism would be immortalized in the 1952 film version.

Meanwhile, 1940 saw a radical change of pace for the amiable actress, as Mrs Danvers (Judith Anderson's most famous screen role) in *Rebecca*. 'I had decided to bypass Danvers, for I abhor unkindness and deliberate cruelty. In the end I did *Rebecca* to demonstrate a degree of personal versatility on the stage.' The following year, it was whimsy again in Noël Coward's hit play *Blithe Spirit*, a ghostly comedy owing something to the popular 'Topper' films. At first, Margaret declined the scene-stealing role of Madame Arcati because she feared it would offend real-life mediums, whom she considered sincere and much maligned. Happily, Coward convinced her that Arcati was a sympathetic depiction.

Rutherford departed the long-running play after one year, partly to make movies like *English Without Tears* (*Her Man Gilbey* in the US) and *The Yellow Canary*. Her role in the latter was originally a one-day job, but her talent to charm helped expand it to three weeks of work. Sir Anthony Asquith, director of their 1943 film *The Demi-Paradise* (US: *Adventure for Two*), said, 'Miss Rutherford is a director's dream. She can improvise inspiredly, she is almost entirely un-camera-conscious, and she is doggedly professional.'

He later revealed, 'Everyone adored working with Margaret, but other than dear Noël, writers never wrote expressly for her ... Her screen roles tended to be peripheral, although of course distinctly unforgettable.'

In 1944 Margaret joined Ivor Novello, Gertrude Lawrence and Jessie Matthews on an ENSA (Entertainments National

Service Association) tour of British airfields and units in Belgium and Normandy. While the other actresses sang or did comic skits, she entertained with her favourite Edward Lear poems, and Novello crooned his new hit song 'We'll Gather Lilacs':

'My dear husband has always been devoted to John Gielgud,' offered Dame Margaret in Mr Davis's smiling presence. 'He admires Sir John more than any living man. But Stringer's favourite song is "We'll Gather Lilacs", and he never allows tea-time to pass without playing it!'

Safely back in England, Margaret co-starred with Sybil Thorndike in *Alice in Wonderland*; they alternated playing the Queen of Hearts and the White Queen. Margaret had to fly during the production. 'It wasn't easy sailing at first. You see, I bounced, and had to acquire the necessary grace, unlike Dame Sybil, who was a most proficient aeronaut. However, once I mastered the knack of exiting and entering the wings on wires, it became quite exhilarating! One of the major thrills of my life, it was, and I always looked forward to my daily flight.'

In 1945 Margaret re-teamed with Novello in his stage extravaganza *Perchance to Dream*. Much later, she allowed, 'If you think about it, as I certainly have, most of my Big Breaks, to coin a phrase, were given to me by gentlemen of the non-heterosexual persuasion, gentlemen who were the leading lights of the theatre and didn't shun my professional services simply because I wasn't comely ... Socially, I was so close to Ivor that Stringer became a bit jealous. Of me, I think, not Ivor! Ivor was the handsomest man in London – even I thought him pretty, and I've never cared a fig for masculine good looks!'

Stringer Davis chimed in, 'I was living with my mother, but I'd known Margaret a long time. We were friends for fifteen years. Then Mum died, and I was left with an empty house filled with furniture and nothing else. So Margaret and I chose to pool our resources, and got married.'

She quietly added, 'Tuft' – her nickname for Davis, whose

hair stood up on top of his head – 'saved me from an old age of loneliness, and I conceivably did the same for him.'

They married in 1945, the year in which Margaret Rutherford became famous, for it was the year *Blithe Spirit* was materialized into an international hit movie. It also made an overseas star of Rex Harrison, who assumed the male lead which author Noël Coward had played on the stage.

'That picture made me recognizable to a majority of people on the street, to people who seldom if ever went to the theatre. It was a tremendous boost to me, finally to attain what everyone called true success …'

Blithe Spirit the movie made Rutherford a character star, but she chose to continue focusing on theatre work. She received several domestic offers of celluloid employment, but 'felt that a picture a year was quite adequate. I was rather disappointed that most of the roles thrown my way were barmy old ladies. The really good and insightful character roles were written for male actors.' As for Hollywood, 'They seldom approached me. As far as they could see, I was the one and only Madame Arcati, but I was the wrong gender, the wrong age and the wrong nationality. As well as the wrong weight, and my question still is, why do they prefer females who resemble yardsticks?'

In 1946 it was back to Wilde territory as Prism in a single matinée performance of *Earnest* for the King George Pension Fund at the Haymarket Theatre. The ever-popular production was booked to tour overseas, but Edith Evans preferred to remain in Britain, and so Margaret Rutherford took up Lady Bracknell for a year, touring Canada and the United States prior to opening on Broadway in March, 1947. Brooks Atkinson praised the star's 'speaking, walking and wearing of costumes, all gathered up into one impression of insufferability'.

In London in 1948 the actress experienced another long-running triumph, as Miss Evelyn Whitchurch in *The*

Happiest Days of Your Life. 'A lovely and lively farce ... I seemed always to represent single ladies, and I suppose this wasn't unusual. I did of course have a marital contract, and still do – gladly – but in my soul I am single and free.'

'We neither one of us dominate the other,' clarified Mr Davis.

Also in 1948, Rutherford filmed her small but pivotal role as Professor Hatton-Jones in the classic *Passport to Pimlico* (the role was first offered to Alastair Sim). It is the professor who verifies documents proving that London's Pimlico is actually a part of the ancient French Duchy of Burgundy. 'I wore a cape, for I always found that a cape greatly helped my characterization. It takes a certain flair to wear a cape, and for me the clothes help create the character. I think I may safely say that I have been more closely identified with wearing capes than anyone else in the movies, except Dracula!'

Co-star Hermione Baddeley disclosed, 'Miss Rutherford was a comic genius who took her roles most seriously, plus she was clever enough to play a part written for a man or somebody, well, older than she was.' Dame Margaret agreed, 'I played men when I was a girl, and as a young woman played middle-aged or elderly females. When was I allowed to play a young lady?

'I was made for middle age, and professional stability only occurred after I entered my fifties. So you see, growing older held no great terror for me, on the contrary it was a relief ... Well, up to a point.'

Rutherford got to confront Alastair Sim in the 1950 movie of *The Happiest Days of Your Life*, about a girls' school forced to share space with a boys' school due to a post-war error by the Ministry of Education's Resettlement Division. 'I was of course Miss Whitchurch, the girls' headmistress. Perhaps the reason I had so much to do with educational characters is that people would come up to me after my performances and tell me they wished they had had a school-teacher like me!'

The boys' headmaster was essayed by Sim, who was not in the play. The film producers wanted a box-office name who could match Rutherford, and both stars were put on their scene-stealing mettle. Offsetting the tweedily sturdy Headmistress's battle of words and wit against pop-eyed Headmaster Pond was the toothy, gangling sportsmistress (Joyce Grenfell). A high point of the comic gem is Margaret Rutherford's unforgettably startled reaction to the boys' school motto, 'Guard Thine Honour'.

At the Savoy she reminisced, 'Miss Whitchurch was one of my favourite stage roles. She has a heart of gold, but is no marshmallow – as they say. I never found any challenge in playing a weak woman … In the end, doing the screen version was worthwhile, but a bit tiresome. Film actors are by nature more competitive and therefore more tiring than stage actors, because film is permanently recorded, while stage actors are usually willing to take turns upstaging each other from night to night.

'During the filming, I had to be very alert to Mr Sim. A most competitive man, although brilliant … Men seem to be particularly competitive with actresses; I don't know if it all boils down to a case of Venus envy?'

In 1950 Rutherford was wheelchair-bound yet aristocratic in Jean Anouilh's *Ring Round the Moon* at the Globe Theatre. In 1952 she experienced the up of the screen's *The Importance of Being Earnest*, directed by Anthony Asquith, and the down of a flop play, *Miss Hargreaves*. The following year she was on top once more, in John Gielgud's production of Congreve's *The Way of the World*, as Lady Wishfort. She was the star attraction for audiences and critics alike, emoting 'with enormous gusto in the grand manner, waving her jaw menacingly and behaving like a splendidly padded windmill, very funny and curiously touching.'

Lighter fare was served up in 1954 in *Alice in Wonderland*, as Rutherford impersonated the White Queen before undertaking Anouilh's *Time Remembered* as an eccentric duchess. 'I did assorted personalities deemed eccentric by the critics, and they are entitled to their opinions. But we should bear in mind that one man's eccentricity is another's routine!'

Kenneth Tynan lauded the British institution in the 1956 revival of *Way of the World*: '[She] is filled with a monstrous vitality – the soul of Cleopatra has somehow got trapped in the corporate shape of an entire lacrosse team. The unique thing about Miss Rutherford is that she can act with her chin alone. Among its many moods I especially cherish the chin commanding, the chin in doubt, and the chin at bay.'

From New York, *Time* magazine observed, 'She is so British that by comparison with her, even John Bull seems the son of a miscegenetic marriage.' Asked why she worked almost exclusively in Britain, Margaret referred to the paucity of Stateside offers, then added, 'I believe strongly in decorum, but I am no prude. The American censors are at times foolishly prudish. When I did a picture titled *Miranda* [1948], the censors in the USA insisted that the mermaid [played by Glynis Johns] could only be allowed a tail if she got married! Most unnatural. It's a wonder they didn't make her wear bloomers!'

As to her continuing good health and energy, she ascribed it to 'breathing deeply. I have sizeable lungs, you know.'

In the 1960s, Rutherford explained, 'I prefer gentle entertainments. I believe that motion pictures should uplift old and young alike. Today's trend to violence for shock value I find deeply distressing. I suppose my sort of pictures – the pictures I appear in – are going out of style.'

Indeed, it's not easy locating some of her titles, though video can be of help. But several Rutherford movies virtually unknown in the US are well worth the effort of seeking out. Even the lesser films are memorably enlivened by the Presence. Who could forget, or not smile at the recollection of *Castle in the Air*, 1952, in which she dons a kilt, a cloak and a beret? Or the 1954 *Aunt Clara*, wherein she inherits a brothel? In the 1954 *Miranda* sequel *Mad About Men*, she chewed the scenery as Nurse Carey, with Stringer Davis as a vicar:

'I liked having Stringer around me, on the set. He saw after everything, from preparing the tea to sewing decorative flowers on to my sandals.' He also cooked (Margaret didn't; she once apprised the press, 'I never travel without my favourite cook') and sometimes sighed, 'I do get tired of playing perfect butlers and dotty clergymen.' Most of the actress's contracts stipulated a token role for her husband.

At the Savoy, Davis recalled, 'Margaret's favourite movie role was probably Prudence Croquet. She was the petshop owner in *An Alligator Named Daisy* [1955].' Rutherford gently interrupted, 'Not my favourite, dear, but one of the most fun. Certainly most intriguing.' She turned to me. 'My reptilian co-star used to let me feel her heartbeat – extraordinary! And I'm convinced that she would smile back at me.'

In 1957 Margaret appeared in *The Smallest Show on Earth*, and in 1959 played a Thatcheresque doyenne of the teacosy in the classic *I'm All Right, Jack*. The social comedy about UK labour relations co-starred Ian Carmichael, Peter Sellers, Terry-Thomas, Richard Attenborough and Dennis Price. America's National Board of Review enshrined it among 1960s' best films.

Despite some bloody movies, the 1960s brought Margaret Rutherford to the pinnacle of her stardom and esteem. She also gained Hollywood-type star treatment via four Miss Marple vehicles for MGM. Not surprisingly, she initially declined the chance to personify Agatha Christie's most famous female sleuth. The reason? Her opposition to crime and murder. Stringer Davis: 'I and others had to talk Margaret into it … The money didn't impress her, though it did me.'

'I don't see eye to eye with Mrs Christie,' intoned Margaret, 'but she is very moralistic. She would be the first to announce that crime does not pay.'

Thus, Margaret starred (with Stringer in more than a token role) in the 1961 *Murder, She Said*. Two years later she reprised Jane in *Murder at the Gallop*, an equine-themed entry co-starring Robert Morley and Flora Robson. The first two were far and away the better films, followed in 1964 by *Murder Most Foul* and in 1965 by *Murder Ahoy*. (Rutherford and Davis did an applause-making cameo in 1965's *The Alphabet Murders*, starring Tony Randall as Christie's Hercule Poirot.)

So it was that in her late sixties and early seventies Margaret Rutherford became Britain's highest-paid actress. She enchanted filmgoers with her Marpleian portrayals, but Mrs Christie struck a sour note when she opined that Rutherford wasn't at all how she pictured Jane, that the actress was too heavy for the part. Margaret later remarked, 'I was a bit hurt, but not terribly. After all, she's not pencil-slim herself, is she?'

To a host of movie-goers, Margaret Rutherford *is* Jane Marple, though subsequent incarnations include Angela Lansbury (whose TV series *Murder, She Wrote* owes partial inspiration to these films), Helen Hayes and, especially, Joan Hickson in the BBC series. Hickson, the closest to Dame Agatha's Marpleian vision, played a small role in *Murder, She Said*.

'I got a tremendous kick out of the part,' recalled Dame Margaret. 'Stringer and I were most always together, and I was treated like royalty. Although the subject was inevitably murder, there was no sensationalism or blood, and the other actors were most pleasant to work with.' Flora Robson pointed out, 'There is nothing actress-y about Margaret. She took to being the star of the piece – a *movie* star – as she did to any task: with gracious responsibility and concern for everyone else.'

In between Marples, Margaret squeezed in some other films, including the 1963 gem *The Mouse on the Moon*. She was the Grand Duchess Gloriana XIII in the space-race spoof featuring wine as rocket-fuel! *Time* called her 'possibly the funniest woman alive'. That same year, she was the penniless, semi-addled Duchess of Brighton in the hit Taylor-Burton vehicle *The VIPs*, earning a Best Supporting Actress Academy Award in 1964. 'Most gratifying ... very encouraging,' she declared, nearly seventy-two at the time. Oscar and eventually the DBE spelled international recognition in capital letters, contrasting with a 1961 incident when she appeared in Danny Kaye's *On the Double*: 'I was sent off to Los Angeles ... Upon arrival, I was to be picked up by a chauffeur. However, the good man had to explain to his superiors that he'd seen nobody waiting who looked remotely like a movie star!'

After her last Christie film, she acted in only three more: Orson Welles's *Chimes at Midnight* (1966; *Falstaff* in the US), *A Countess From Hong King* (sharing her bed scenes with a menagerie of stuffed animals), and *Arabella*, delightful if incredible as an Italian beauty's aunt!

The actress didn't abandon stagework during the 1960s, but ironically, at the same time that she reached her professional peak, the end of her memory and good health were in sight, and would cost her first her theatrical and then her screen career.

Stagewise, in 1957 she reprised *Earnest* in Dublin, and in that and the following year toured Australia as Miss Whitchurch in *The Happiest Days of Your Life* and the duchess in *Time Rembered*. In 1959 and 1960 she played Minerva Goody in *Farewell, Eugene* in London and New York. By then, theatre-goers would line up around the block to see her in almost anything. Nevertheless, John Gielgud's 1961 *Dazzling Prospect* was a relative failure at London's Globe. *Plays and Players* noted, 'Whether an individual enjoyed it or not depended entirely on whether or not he liked Margaret Rutherford. If he did, then it was a play which suited her to the full, and a cast backed up admirably her every eccentricity. If he did not, then no effort of director or cast could have mitigated the boredom. Evidently a lot of people did not.' The star humbly reasoned, 'People in London are used to me. In other English-speaking venues, they don't see me as often, and consequently they imagine I'm quite wonderful.'

In 1962 she again indulged in Restoration comedy, as Mrs Candour in *The School for Scandal* at the Haymarket. Caryl Brahms wrote, 'She does not merely get her laughs, she acts for them and can be (even though it is not called for here) heartbreaking as well as so funny it hurts.'

Motion pictures absorbed more of her time, and she did not return to the stage until May 1965. By then, she had suffered a serious nervous breakdown and was living in a nursing home. Each night, a doctor accompanied her to the Saville Theatre, where she starred in the American comedy *The Solid Gold Cadillac*, as Laura Partridge, the role played on screen in the 1950s by Judy Holliday. In 1966 she was back at the Haymarket in Sheridan's *The Rivals* as Mrs Malaprop. It was her final play, and a disheartening experience, for her memory was failing her. Many of the malapropisms were her own; she informed the press: 'As in all comedy, the timing had to be precise. Catch the split second and the laughs come. Miss two beats and they are gone. Sensing the timing in a period piece is always difficult, but combining a crop of malapropisms with this was very wearying.'

Insiders said that all her life Margaret had feared losing her memory on the stage, and now that it had happened, she would have to be content with movies. Sadly, while filming *Arabella* in Rome, she fell and broke her hip, and had to withdraw from *The Song of Norway* and decline *The Virgin and the Gypsy*. Her health never fully recovered. She told Noël Coward, 'I have good spells, when my spirits are high, but my biggest disappointment is never being quite well enough to work. I am not insurable for motion picture contracts.'

For a time, she shuttled between hospitals – visited by the

likes of Prime Minister Edward Heath – and her and Stringer's beloved home, Elm Close, which hospital and nursing bills later forced them to sell. As her mobility decreased – even though neither she nor Stringer had ever learned how to drive – her spirits darkened, and she wondered to friends if her faulty memory might decline into a loss of her mind.

Stringer explained, 'Today I engaged two lesbian nurses. They can lift her in and out of their little car with ease and take her for rides.' The duo's friends felt that without Stringer, Margaret's will to live might have been eroded. Sybil Thorndike, with whom Stringer corresponded after Margaret's death, believed, 'He was less her husband than her best friend and invaluable amanuensis. He made her life easy, or as easy as it could be, and she had his complete loyalty.'

During our interview, Dame Margaret admitted, 'Those last several pictures I did, of course I enjoyed doing them. They were the jam, as it were, of my career ... I only wish Aunt Bessie could have seen the sets and marvelled at the amount I was paid, and attended the premières. But I doubt I would have done those pictures without Stringer along.'

Which, I asked, were her favourite roles and which ones did she regret having missed out on?

'I loved Lady Wishfort in *The Way of the World*. People said my Wishfort was almost lecherous, and I think I served Congreve's and Gielgud's intentions well ... Wilde is a favourite playwright and a pleasure to perform; I only wish I had done his lesser-known works. Among my picture characterizations, I feel a special kinship with Arcati, and I admired Jane Marple's determination to ferret out wrongdoers.

'Too many characters I would love to have tried – far too many to mention. To name the one which does come to mind: the elderly woman in *The Whisperers*,' for which Edith Evans was Oscar-nominated as Best Actress.

Back when female directors were a distinct anomaly,

Margaret Rutherford had hopes of becoming a stage director. 'I liked everything about the theatre. What is that expression? "The smell of the greasepaint and the roar of the crowd." I was having difficulty establishing myself as an actress, and for a while I entertained thoughts of directing. Those were soon crushed, for it was all I could manage to secure work as an actor, and once I did, I had to spend much time getting new parts.'

Stringer Davis asserted, 'The theatre establishment which Margaret so strove to become a part of was very shortsighted in appreciating her special talents. They only judged books by their covers. But Margaret made the long, hard climb with unflagging good cheer and without bitterness. As I often tell her, she really is a blithe spirit …'

After her passing on 22 May 1972, Dame Margaret Rutherford's tombstone was engraved with the words 'Blithe Spirit'. Stringer was quoted, 'I can tell you I have never been in a taxi with Margaret where the driver would accept a fare. She was so universally loved.' Though seven years her junior, he died the next year, and was buried with a treasured letter from John Gielgud in his pyjama pocket, its contents unknown. Gielgud stated, 'I have known them both as a couple and as individuals, and it truly can be said that they were sweetly civilized people.'

11

Dame Sybil Thorndike

*I was told it would be 'exceedingly' tough to meet Dame
Sybil Thorndike, let alone interview her. 'Connections,' I
was advised ... I had one: actor-dancer-wit Sir Robert
Helpmann. And so I met the Dame – since 1931 – at the
Green Park apartment of a mutual friend of hers and Sir
Robert's. Nearly ninety, she was sharp in both senses of the
word, yet patient, even tutorial. She smiled seldom, except
when speaking of her late husband, actor-director Sir Lewis
Casson (1876-1969)* or her signature performance, Saint
Joan.

'It was a splendid occasion,' said Dame Sybil of the
400th anniversary of Shakespeare's birth in 1964.
'The Queen gave a reception [for theatre actors]. It
was *tout le monde*,' with guests like Edith Evans, Flora
Robson and Margaret Rutherford. 'It was a splendid chance
to celebrate the Bard and to remember. Memorable roles
and events ... Shakespeare in our training and apprenticeship. Doing the minor roles, the major roles. Good notices
and indifferent ones ...So many memories. A flood of
memories, and each of us actresses having shared more or

167

less the same world-famous roles which he wrote.'

A slight pause. 'Or purportedly wrote.' A discreet cough.

The authorship of Shakespeare's plays has been a literary 'mystery' for centuries. What was Dame Sybil's opinion on the subject? She was careful: 'There are ... similarities to some of Christopher Marlowe's work. Marlowe died young, so there is another puzzle ... The *fait accompli* of the genius of one Shakespearian play after another. How he rose from anonymity to a sudden prominence ... The mysteries of his personal identity. Was he one man or a symbol? It takes on almost a mystical quality. But speculation is idleness. What is beyond questioning is the immortality of the plays in the Shakespearian canon.'

The actress famed for her talent, longevity and perfect posture bemoaned the diminution of classical training among aspiring young actors. 'That is entirely the point. You call them "aspiring", but too much aspiration is the same thing as ambition. No more, no less – ambitious greed. My contemporaries sought to become actors. No one thought to become a *star*. If notoriety or acclaim lies in one's future, then there it is. Like a flower, it will unfold in due time.

'I realize now there is television. We have motion pictures. Money abounds, and it stimulates greed ... There is no substitute for performing the great plays and trying the great roles, and it begins not with greatness, but humility. Force of personality or looks or naked ambition do not – or should not – create a bridge to some imagined stardom.'

Dame Sybil firmly held that the classics (by then including once modern playwrights like Coward and Rattigan) were the bedrock of an actor's education. 'Experimental plays have their place. One does not experiment with becoming an actor. Experiments are for the bored or unchallenged actor. First one becomes an actor, a steady and slow process ...'

Agnes Sybil Thorndike was born in Gainsborough, Lincolnshire, in 1882, the eldest of four. 'It is luck, being the eldest. It is power, in that early stage of life. It can instil a modest ambition ... There's the other side of it, the having to be responsible at an early age. I always felt or was made to feel that I had to set others an example.'

Sybil's siblings all went into the theatre, though minus the quantity or quality which transported their elder to Olympus. (Likewise, her four children and several of her grandchildren took up acting.) 'I may have had or done that little something extra,' she theorized. Sybil bowed on the amateur stage at the age of four, and by seven was starring in a melodrama titled *The Dentist's Cure* which she and her brother Russell had written. Its subtitle was the *Sweeney Todd*-ish *Saw Their Silly Heads Off!*

Dame Sybil readily acknowledged 'my attraction to Grand Guignol. I remember that several of my colleagues chose to pity Miss Davis and Miss Crawford for their movie *Whatever Happened To Baby Jane?*. Possibly they envied their salaries. But I thought what wonderful gusto they showed in their performances! It must have been pleasant work. Easily more so than the part of a typical lady 'of a certain age', to use the French expression ... Some of the less imaginative playwrights thought of me solely in terms of respectable old ladies. Characters who witness conflict but are dull in themselves.'

The fact that Sybil's mother was a first-rate pianist nudged the would-be actress towards music. She dutifully attempted to become a pianist and even battled piano-cramp until her efforts did not seem worth it and the family urged her back to her original ambition of acting. Mrs Thorndike arranged for her daughter to audition for Charles Wyndham. It did not happen; the girl suddenly fell very ill, continued her schooling, then in 1904, almost twenty-two, finally had a Big Audition.

Its outcome was that she joined Ben Greet's company. Her professional début was in *The Palace of Truth*, and later that year she and her fellow Greet-ers set sail for America, where they toured for two years. 'The comfort, and even luxury, which we now associate with the States wasn't wide-spread then. There were several primitive places, and a lack of amenities which I'm sure I hope I've forgotten. With respect, but it was a joy when at last we returned to civilization.'

During her Yankee apprenticeship, Sybil performed over a hundred roles. They included Lucianus, nephew to the king (*Hamlet*), Ophelia, Gertrude, Rosalind, Helena, Nerissa and Everyman. When the grinding schedule and bumpy transport overcame some of the older or more pampered actresses, Sybil went on in their place. 'Acting,' she enunciated, 'requires *energy*.'

By 1907 Sybil was with the Play Actors' Society in London. In a farce called *The Marquis* she played a young American. 'It was the only performance of this play, so what happened was most extraordinary.' What happened was that the world's greatest living playwright, George Bernard Shaw, was in the audience. The next day, he inquired whether Miss Thorndike might care to understudy in a revival of *Candida*.

'For the fabled Bernard Shaw, most any actor or actress would have sold his soul to Faust,' grinned the actress for whom Shaw created *Saint Joan*.

What was Shaw really like?

'He was an enigma. Even unto himself … What he knew, he knew very well. He was an unusually intelligent and curious man. But what he didn't know, he stayed away from, and what didn't interest him, he entirely dismissed from his mind.

'As a playwright, he was second only to Shakespeare … Naturally, I owe him a continual thanks, for *Saint Joan*, which is the one role I am absolutely, lastingly associated with. It's true that we performers like to be known for our diverse talents and the variety of our roles. Yet if a performer is very lucky, he will be associated with one really outstanding role, which he has made his through timing and talent.

'Shaw took me under his wing. He was as fatherly towards

me as I think he could be towards any other human being. His psychology was complex ... He was not easy to get to know. But as a dramatist, he is unmatched in this century.'

Thorndike appeared in the 1941 film of Shaw's 1905 social comedy *Major Barbara*, starring Wendy Hiller as the idealistic Barbara Undershaft (she'd previously starred in Shaw's *Pygmalion*). Dame Sybil recalled, 'We were a splendid cast, directed by Shaw's trusted associate, Gabriel Pascal. Wendy Hiller, Rex Harrison, Robert Morley, Emlyn Williams ... I believe Deborah Kerr made her film début, and I remember that Robert, who was only a few years older than Wendy, played Wendy's father.

'He complained about it minimally. It is easier, technically and egotistically, to play older than younger ... A few snide reviewers intimated that I was rather long in the tooth to keep portraying Joan of Arc. When one plays younger, the audience strains to see if you look the part. When one plays older, one has their sympathy and their admiration – no one ever invokes vanity when an actor plays older.

'Bette Davis once came around to tea. She said that playing older was one of the reasons she was so admired as a film actress. But it did have one drawback, and that was that people thought one must be absolutely ancient. Fans would tell her she was awfully well-preserved, because they'd seen her portraying middle-aged characters several decades before!'

Speaking of stars, Dame Sybil often shared the stage or screen with a fellow luminary, frequently in a lesser or dowdier role. As in 1951, when she co-starred in London with Edith Evans in *The Waters of the Moon*, playing an elderly lady in a sweater to Evans's glamorous cynosure (as Wendy Hiller did in the 1978 revival with Ingrid Bergman). 'Certain onlookers expected fireworks between Edith and myself. Others thought we might go at it in a subtle fashion, undermining or upstaging one another. We confounded them all by getting along very nicely.

'Edith got the nice wardrobe and the role which in the

wrong hands could have been overdone. She was perfect. I got the cardigan, and praise for portraying a character who bottles up much of her emotion. Technically, it is easier to portray someone who is flamboyant than one who is repressed ... It was a wonderful experience. An overlooked play.'

Dame Sybil got to play royalty in the 1957 film *The Prince and the Showgirl*, adapted by Terence Rattigan from his somewhat airy play *The Sleeping Prince*. It involves an American showgirl and a lusty prince, during George V's 1911 coronation. The Marilyn Monroe Production was helmed by Laurence Olivier. Actress-producer and actor-director did not get along. Olivier openly insulted Monroe to the press, and their attempt at chemistry falls flat on the screen.

'It was a somewhat acrimonious situation,' stated the diplomatic veteran actress. 'From my point of view, it was glamorous. I was the Queen Dowager. I wore a magnificent tiara, of course. Miss Monroe was a lady-in-waiting to me. There wasn't overmuch of a plot, and little tension by Terence's usual standards ... Miss Monroe was sweet to me, at first overawed but later curious about my career and acting.

'She displayed a healthy curiosity, and I commended her for trying to guide her own projects, as Hollywood had not done well by her.

'If she could have done more theatre, she might have survived her career and her reputation as a low-comedienne. She told me, sadly, that one of her screen directors had wanted her to appear in a remake of Maugham's *Of Human Bondage* [which made a dramatic star of Bette Davis]. She would have done it with James Dean, but the studio vetoed. They said her "type" was at odds with such a dramatic and unsympathetic character.'

And so, Sybil Thorndike went to Belfast to perform in Shaw's *Candida* and *Widower's Houses*. In the latter, a young actor named Lewis Casson played Trench. In 1908 the two wed, and in 1923 Shaw wrote *Saint Joan* for Thorndike, 'a woman of noble mien'. Meanwhile, she joined the repertory company at Manchester's Gaiety. 'Miss Horniman, who was in charge, was an admirer of Shaw and used to put on his plays. By the time I left her, I felt well-trained in Shakespeare and Shaw. Naturally, the young always feel themselves to be well-trained.'

Sybil then joined the company at the Duke of York's in London, and went to America to tour and appear on Broadway in W. Somerset Maugham's *Smith*. 'Your generation, and your parents', have more or less forgotten that before he became a prolific and amply paid novelist, Maugham was a London playwright of the first water. We lost him to Hollywood …'

In 1912 Sybil was back with Miss Horniman in Manchester, a leading actor with her company – its plays sometimes helmed by Casson – until the outbreak of the First World War. With war, the couple and their three children moved to London. He joined the army, she joined the Old Vic at Lilian Baylis's invitation. For four years she 'luxuriated' in Shakespeare's finest, that is to say, Portia, Lady Macbeth, Rosalind, Beatrice, Ophelia and *King Lear*'s Fool (male actors were at a premium during the war years).

A critic for the *Sunday Times* prophesied, 'Miss Thorndike will be a great actress, so long as she learns to keep her hands beneath her shoulders.'

I asked Dame Sybil her philosophy of dramatic criticism: 'They are a necessary … well, "evil" is too strong a word. Most of the time …'

Then came Sybil's Greek period. In 1919 and 1920 she was Hecuba in Euripides' *Trojan Women*, then tackled *Medea*. Next, a two-year stint at the Little Theatre in assorted Grand Guignol melodramas. Sybil and brother Russell co-starred with Lewis, who directed, in such offerings as *Fear*, *The Hound of Death* and *The Kill*. During the Roaring Twenties, audiences could publicly attend fright-sessions which during the Victorian and Edwardian eras would have been condemned as 'morbid'. In *The Old Ladies*, Sybil chilled audiences by having her eyes gouged out by a fellow inmate at an insane asylum – with knitting needles!

'It was not hurtful ... amusing in its macabre way. Audiences then were more innocent than today. Crime was not as rampant. Violence was far more controlled, although don't forget that there were always true villains. We English have produced spine-tingling murderers. Very individual ones like Jack the Ripper ... or Christie or our various Bluebeards ...'

When horror lost its box-office appeal, Thorndike and Casson took over the New Theatre, opening with *The Cenci*. Shaw attended a performance and was inspired to write *Saint Joan*. Before *Joan*'s première in 1924, Sybil had made her film début in *Moth and Rust*, in 1921.

'At the outset, I was pleased to be in something as novel or daring as moving pictures ... I did a number of shorts – classical extracts' (*Macbeth, Merchant of Venice, Lady of the Camellias, Esmeralda, The Scarlet Letter*, etc.). Most were in 1922. During *Saint Joan*, she avoided the cinema, returning in 1927 to shoot a Shavian extract.

'I did a picture here, a picture there. I would stay away for years at a time. I found that photographed images couldn't compare to the stage. Not for the spectator, and not for this performer ... Let us admit, I was too old to hurl myself into a career as a screen vamp. A screen actress had to be a vamp, or a little girl, like Miss Pickford. I had too many seasons and too little patience to be either.'

In 1957, when Otto Preminger filmed *Saint Joan*, he cast nineteen-year-old newcomer Jean Seberg as the Frenchwoman who died at the stake at nineteen in 1431. Sybil came to the role at forty-one. Opening at the New Theatre in March 1924, *Saint Joan* ran 244 performances, but Thorndike revived it regularly, in Britain and abroad, until March 1941. The play/role was the climax of her career. In the 1970s she smilingly noted: 'I felt that I never wanted to do anything else, that I'd reached something I could never reach again, and I was just so grateful that the audience was there night

Sybil Thorndike as Shaw's *Saint Joan*, 1924.

Dame Sybil in the 1949 play *Treasure Hunt*.

Dame Sybil and Marilyn Monroe in *The Prince and the Showgirl*, 1957.

(*above left*) Estelle Winwood, leading lady of Broadway and the West End.

(*above*) A 1955 portrait of Estelle Winwood.

Winwood, aged 93, in her final film, *Murder by Death*, 1976.

after night to see me do it.' About filming an extract, she felt, 'It was, remember, only a portion … I don't believe that the greatest stage plays can be adequately represented on the screen. I think it cheats the audience, and the playwright besides. My own feelings of victory in the part were always on the stage.'

Of the movie version, she preferred to say 'next to nothing. What I had to say, I said to John Gielgud [who was in the film], and once was enough.'

Dame Sybil noted, 'Joan's story was not written down until some three hundred years after her death. She is one of history's most intriguing figures. Enigmatic. There is much to delve into, but it can never be known. She wore men's clothing even before she led the army; she was a gentle, rather odd soul who was fierce in battle. What Freud would have made of her, I can only guess! Naturally, once she became not only a heroine but, in many eyes, a saint, the truth was further obscured.'

About the age difference, 'I thought more about it as the years wore on. I had misgivings. Audiences didn't seem to. So I went by what audiences wanted … What matters with Joan is her passion, and also her being so different. Not how she looks. You may believe me when I say that, portraying Joan, I did not feel my years, I felt much younger. I felt *her* years.'

Apart from Joan, the 1920s and 1930s were Thorndike's heyday, in which she presented one classical – and sometimes a modern – role after another, often directed by her husband. 'Memory suggests that I worked non-stop.' In 1928 and 1929, she toured South Africa in a variety of roles including Joan, and in 1930 she co-starred in Paul Robeson's *Othello*, then alternated Shakespeare, Shaw, the Greeks, Ibsen, Beaumont and Fletcher, toured Australia in 1932, co-starred with Emlyn Williams as Miss Moffat in 1938 in his *The Corn Is Green*, then spent 1940-2 touring Welsh mining villages and towns as Lady Macbeth, Medea and Candida.

'It was richly rewarding. Most of these audiences had never

seen another actress in the roles ...

'Let me see ... *Saint Joan* wasn't the only Shaw play. I did *Captain Brassbound's Conversion*. In the mid-1930s I was in Noël Coward's *Hands Across the Sea*. Not a success – surprising, for him – and so, a long time until we recombined our efforts ... In 1945 I was the Nurse in *Uncle Vanya*, and about twenty years later I did the picture version,' her last film, in 1963.

'I cannot think of any substantial roles I did not do. Jocasta in *Oedipus [Rex]* ... I was the wife of the American President Woodrow Wilson [in *In Time to Come* by Howard Koch and John Huston], I was Mrs Whyte in *Waters of the Moon* ...Oh, and the tours – the foreign tours ...'

After the war, in her sixties, her career suffered a change. 'But you see, the world changed. Almost everything changed after the second big war.' In London, Dame Sybil was mostly relegated to drawing-room comedies. 'I like to laugh, yes. But comedy, it's best left to comics.' She recreated her classic roles, sometimes dramatic highlights from given plays, during lengthy tours of Australia and South Africa. She also performed international poetry recitals with her husband.

In 1960 she appeared in Noël Coward's fiftieth play, his first to be declined by H.M. Tennent, the management that had presented nearly all his West End plays since the Second World War. Instead, *Waiting in the Wings* was presented under the auspices of Coward's friend Michael Redgrave. It was about a group of elderly actresses living in retirement at a home called The Wings. The thespians' attitudes range from bitterness to hope to resignation. Sir Noël felt, 'It contains the basic truth that old age needn't be nearly so dreary and sad as it's supposed to be, provided you greet it with humour and live it with courage.'

Wings co-starred Lewis Casson, and audiences greeted it enthusiastically, but critics generally slaughtered it. They lambasted the veteran playwright for not being part of the new wave of 'angry young man' writer-agitators. 'They were beastly,' sniffed Dame Sybil. 'Probably nervous about the play's theme, old age. Yet it happens to all of us – if we're lucky.'

She added, 'Audiences liked the play. Then they read the critics, and most stopped coming. A bunch of sheep!' Even so, *Wings*, Coward's most underrated comedy, lasted nine months on the boards, in and out of London.

In 1962 the great Dame took part in a short-lived musical of *Vanity Fair*, noting, 'Never be sorry to attempt something new – never, never, never.' The following year, she and Sir Lewis acted in Olivier's *Uncle Vanya*, helping to open the National Theatre at the Old Vic:

'In ... 1944 I joined the Olivier–Richardson Old Vic season at the New. I was Margaret to Larry's Richard III, Aase to Ralph's Peer Gynt ... and other superb roles. It's not until after seventy or thereabouts that people covertly begin trying to tell you to retire. They want you to think you're straining yourself if you appear on a stage. It's idiotic how many people that should know better believe this.'

In 1966, Dame Sybil and Sir Lewis (six years her senior) made their farewell joint appearance in London in *Arsenic and Old Lace*. 'A charming play, and appropriate to end with laughter, nicely mixed with the macabre,' she smiled in recollection. Six months after Casson's death in early 1969, she made her final appearance, at the Thorndike Theatre in Leatherhead. In 1970 she was made a Companion of Honour, the highest award which a monarch can bestow upon an actress.

Obliquely referring to her lifemate of sixty-one years, Dame Sybil allowed, 'I could have consciously or unconsciously decided to dry up, mentally, physically ... Except for Lewis, I was typically the oldest person in any group I was ever in. Never did I think of age as a drawback or burden.' Casson had lived to ninety-three, and Thorndike's family has admitted that the matriarch was determined to match his lifespan and surpass it: 'She had a will of iron,' said one daughter-in-law. 'A star not only of the stage, but of life,' said A.P. Herbert. Olivier declared, 'She does not need a vehicle in which to shine; she is a beacon and a magnet in her daily life.'

At sixty-five, she commenced her autobiography, quoting Benvenuto Cellini, 'Everyone should write one book. A record of a life must always hold the interest – there is no life that's dull, no life without some sign of growth, and a thing grown or growing holds in it some excitement.' She reasoned, 'The book may be for no one but myself, for in the writing of it there is a tidying up of my inner affairs … a sort of confession.'

But the memoirs were never even half-completed, as she was too busy living out decade after decade. She wrote mostly about her antecedents and their Victorian lives. She recounted how her father's father's first wife left him for a younger, more appealing man. 'This was a terrible blow to the General … Never was the erring wife's name mentioned again … She was as dead. I believe her children never heard of her again.' The *Beginnings of an Autobiography* appeared in *My Dear One*, a posthumous book about the courtship of Sybil's parents.

'I did have a colourful family,' she proudly informed me. 'Few will acknowledge that the Victorian era was a time of much change and progress, compared to what had gone before it.' Her father's half-brother's daughter Emily, Thorndike pointed out, 'became a renowned professional singer and changed her surname to Hart-Dyke. Some of my feminine relations confounded and exceeded all expectations', including the speaker!

Dame Sybil's screen career pales beside her theatrical legend. Her most often seen movie is *The Prince and the Showgirl*, in which she was seventy-five and not at her varied or histrionic best. She once confided in Noël Coward that she would love to have reprised some of her stage roles on the silver screen. For instance, Kitty in Maugham's *The*

Painted Veil, taken over two years later by Greta Garbo in 1934. Sir Noël asserted: 'There are stage goddesses who seduce from a distance. Their voices, mannerisms and fire light up the stage. Think of Tallulah Bankhead, Sybil Thorndike, Ethel Merman ... a long list. However, for one reason or another they cannot translate their stage appeal to celluloid. Proportion is one factor; in close-up, an actress's face may not be pleasing enough, or in close-up, her personality may overpower. Or she may simply require the spark of a live audience, to ignite.'

Thorndike confessed, 'I minded about good grooming and hygiene. But as a clergyman's daughter I was not urged to cultivate prettiness or vanity ... I was often told I seemed older than my age, and the looking-glass informed me that I was neither lithe nor winsome. The females of my family were blessed with character rather than beauty.'

Even so, Dame Sybil's is a disarming presence on film, particularly as well-rounded characters. She is less memorable as such stock British characters as, say, duchesses, lacking a Margaret Rutherford's comic élan or sense of whimsy. In 1928 Sybil excelled as Nurse Edith Cavell in *Dawn*, directed by Herbert Wilcox (Dame Anna Neagle's husband). 'It was a great responsibility to enact such a famous and honoured lady.' In 1947's *Nicholas Nickleby* she was Mrs Squeers. 'Dickens can be a trap. Too easy, if one goes over the top and makes his characters caricatures.'

Working for Alfred Hitchcock in *Stage Fright* (1950, starring Marlene Dietrich and Jane Wyman) was 'highly informative. He made it painfully clear that the motion picture is a director's medium, more than an actor's. He was precise, aloof and polite rather than helpful. Gave few directions; I took it as his showing confidence in his performers, though.'

She worked for Wilcox again in *The Lady With the Lamp*, a Neagle vehicle about Florence Nightingale. Two years later, in 1953, she was Queen Victoria in Lewis Milestone's

Melba. 'It is an undeniable thrill to do either Victoria or Elizabeth I, for they were so palpably human, terribly influential and our two greatest sovereigns.'

Incredibly – or not – Thorndike was only of brief interest to Hollywood. That was when talkies came in, and because of her cultural renown and expertly cultivated voice. Again, age was the mitigating factor. Nor did she care to carve out a lucrative if undemanding career as token Britannic aristocrats, biddies and fusspots. She was dedicated to her family, to raising her offspring in England and to working whenever possible with her husband. 'As I grew older, I discovered that respect among moviemakers tends to mean they give you the smallest roles,' she said of most of her 1950s and 1960s screen parts.

I requested Dame Sybil to offer the following thumbnail impressions of a few of her co-workers:

Paul Robeson. 'In Britain, we liked him. Very much. In the States in those days, they couldn't see past his colour or his liberal politics. Or past the rather amazing fact that a coloured man should hold political views.'

Olivier. 'We all know and praise Larry ... But he is also an athlete of the first rank. He loved to leap about, to scream, to play the dashing youth or the wild man. His Othello was quite as good as Robeson's.'

Edith Evans. 'So versatile. Energetic. Terribly sweet. A perfectionist.'

John Gielgud. 'Marvellous actor, marvellous director ... As has been said, he is an even finer actor than Larry, at least from the neck up.'

Michael Wilding. 'We did *Stage Fright*, and he was a top-rank film star here. Then he decided to move to Hollywood, and immediately his roles reflected a decline in quality. After all, we are foreigners over there ...'

Dame Wendy Hiller. 'She has improved with age, and that is a compliment on top of a compliment. She was Shaw's favourite actress – on the screen.'

Shaw's favourite stage actress died on 9 June 1976, after

two heart attacks in four days. Three weeks before, she had succeeded in outliving her husband. At her Westminster Abbey memorial service, John Gielgud called her 'The most loved actress since [his aunt] Ellen Terry.' Robert Morley's son Sheridan said, 'One might add also the best.'

12

Estelle Winwood

'I was born in Lee, England, a very long time ago. Don't ask me in what year! It doesn't matter in the least,' said the seemingly frail but indomitable Estelle Winwood. The actress was so old, she was almost awesome – seventy-one years older than myself – and one feared contradicting or angering her, as if it might have injured her health. Yet she was stronger than she looked. Obviously. And not fond of interviews. We met in 1973 at a party, where Winwood said of a seventy-ish woman, 'She has a lot of go in her, doesn't she?' Estelle was herself ninety at the time. I interviewed her in 1976 on the occasion of her latest and final film. We kept in touch until her death in 1984, at the age of 101.

'If you have done your homework, which I doubt, because you're so young,' stated Estelle Winwood, crotchety and barely smiling, 'you're aware that I starred in the first play ever to win a Pulitzer Prize.' She paused, fixing me with her gimlet eye. I racked my memory.

'Was it –?'

She interrupted before I could guess wrong. Or right.

'*Why Marry?*' she announced.

The comedy in three acts bowed on 25 December 1917, and ran 120 performances at the Astor Theatre. It concerned a young scientist too poor to wed his thoroughly modern lab technician, played by Winwood. Willing to wed and continue working, she then agrees to live with him outside matrimony. Of course, in the end the pair must marry, for, 'Bad as marriage is, until we reform it, it is the best we have to offer.'

'It was rather clever,' recalled the actress some six decades later. 'Somebody named Jesse Lynch Williams wrote it, I remember that. All the American critics were behind it. They said it was America's answer to Bernard Shaw. Wanted to prove American playwrights could be clever and witty too. That may be why they gave it a Pulitzer Prize, because no one ever revives it. Or probably even remembers it, except me.'

The bird-like thespian glossed over the fact that she had also appeared in plays by Shaw, Masefield and Galsworthy, directed by those playwrights themselves. Off the screen, she was most closely identified with comedies by Coward, Barrie and Wilde, and she preferred to discuss the people she knew rather than the works in which she'd performed. 'People are the interesting thing,' she said with asperity. 'A play or a picture is all right, but it's here today and gone tomorrow. It comes hard to lose all the people I've cared about,' she admitted, not finding it particularly cheering to 'be considered an antique'.

Because of her 'advanced age and limited attention span; I bore rather easily,' a session with Ms Winwood was never a long one. She said that 'if at all possible', she'd rather answer one question or two at a time in writing, usually by having a friend take down her comments about a given co-worker, then mailing them to this interviewer. 'Are you certain you want my opinions on so many things and people?' she wondered. 'I don't want to enervate your readers via boredom ...'

There was small chance of that, for the actress was always an outspoken personality, tremendously under-used by Hollywood. She became a celebrity in spite of the movies and her own qualms, plus what she had once viewed as a physical flaw – her eyes. Schoolmates had nicknamed her 'Cow Eyes', but later she proclaimed, 'My advice to actresses is don't worry about your looks. The very thing that makes you unhappy in your appearance may be the one thing to make you a star.'

An actress for nearly a century, Estelle was born 24 January 1883, the daughter of a civil engineer. Asked about growing up in the Victorian era, she allowed, 'The clothes were different, mostly. Other than that, much depended on your parents. My family was strict. Very strict. No one else in my family ever went on the stage, except in the Shakespearian sense ('All the world's a stage ...'). Appearances were vital.

'One had to look and act virginal, whether or not one was. I of course was. Today, one has to dress like a fallen woman, even if one isn't ... Don't ask me to recreate a time that was so long ago I can only dimly remember it.'

Estelle made her stage début in 1888 at five. At six, she told the press in 1968, she decided to become an actress after seeing an equestrienne with long and golden but thin hair at a circus. 'I have thin hair, so I decided to become an actress too.' Educated at Ealing, she studied at the Lyric Stage Academy and at the Liverpool Repertory Theatre, where she acted in over a hundred plays in three years.

'I've always been fit. Always took my health for granted. I don't have the patience to fret over it or to refrain from doing things I like.'

In 1898 she made her professional début at the Theatre Royal in Manchester, with Sir John Hare, as Laura in Tom Robertson's *School*. Soon after, she bowed in London, then spent several years touring with Hare's company. She enjoyed triumphs in several Galsworthy plays and in Shaw's

Arms and the Man: 'Shaw used to say to us, "Don't act – say my lines." '

She wrote me about Shaw, 'We have something in common. It got to the point where he became rather notorious for having lived so long, as I have done ... He said to us once that he'd been asked the advantages of growing old. He'd paused a great while, then said, "There are none." After another pause, he said, "Except when you consider the alternative."

'Mr Shaw was born old. I was not ... He was rumoured to be neutral about sex. I certainly couldn't say whether he was celibate, or only said it to shock. I'd like to know what Freud might have thought of him ... Shaw would have made a perfect priest, except he happened to be an atheist.'

She declared of three other fabled playwrights:

'Somerset Maugham was rather like this new painter, Andrew (*sic*) Warhol. Courting fame at any price ... He tried to be modern and daring in his plays. I should know – I was in some of them. The result was, he's very outmoded today. I don't think they do his plays any more. He wanted to write what he thought would sell. He wanted to get fame quickly, and he did, but who remembers him now? A very pretentious man.'

J.M. Barrie. 'He was a complete Victorian. Very inhibited – a maiden gentleman, if you understand that rather subtle term. This may explain why all his stories are so outmoded today ... When we filmed *Quality Street*, ages ago [1937], it was a rather big event in Hollywood – a film from Barrie. But it lost out completely, and now I don't think you could pay Hollywood to film any of his stories except that bloody *Peter Pan*.'

Terence Rattigan. 'Didn't like his writing. Old-fashioned – like Noël Coward, but minus the humour.'

She did befriend Coward, who dubbed her, oddly enough, 'an ageless Victorian Venus'. 'He was a nice man. Had excellent manners. He knew how to treat a lady. But always working too hard at being teddibly, teddibly successful ... I abandoned all that long ago. I decided that if success is going to be defined for you by others, then I wouldn't play that game.

'After all, no matter how popular you may be, somebody else is bound to be more popular, more pretty, younger, etc., etc. For me, success equals being happy most or much of the time. If you have that, you are a success.

'I've found that if you always need to chase others and obtain their good opinions of your career, you will forever be frustrated. Buy a cat or a dog instead – they make much better pets than critics or fans.'

In Liverpool and elsewhere, Winwood starred as Nora in *A Doll's House* and in plays like *The Admirable Crichton* and *A Woman of No Importance*. In London, she did an estimated eighty plays. When I inquired how many plays her entire career numbered, she feigned exhaustion. 'Oh, too bloody many to remember! Hundreds and hundreds – more or less.'

In 1916 she journeyed to New York. 'It was during that abominable war which was so soon forgotten, and still is. For those of us born early in this century or before it, the first international war was much the worst for the English. It was a trauma and a tragedy. A tragedy, because we lost a generation of young men and because two decades later we were senselessly repeating the same thing, with more sophisticated weapons.'

In New York, she made her Broadway bow as Lucilla in *Hush* at the Little Theatre. She was an instant hit, and decided 'to stop', performing in 'melodramas and classics and everything in between'. Her plays ranged from *Too Many Husbands* – 'That title is the story of my life!' – and *A Successful Calamity* to *The Taming of the Shrew* and *Trelawny of the Wells*. She ran over a year in *Spring Cleaning* on Broadway in 1923-4, starred in Noël Coward's *Fallen Angels* in 1927, then in 1928 appeared in *The Furies* for director George Cukor:

'We worked together before he went to Hollywood. We remained on rather friendly terms, probably because we didn't keep working together. As a man, he was a lamb. As a director, a lion – with a lot of pride.'

Cukor was quoted as saying, 'Estelle made the graceful transition from a beautiful leading lady to a beautiful character actress and finally a beautiful relic.' As to her looks, Winwood advised *Photoplay*, 'Beauty is just an opinion. But I am undeniably slim and dress well, and that counts for rather a lot. Especially in Hollywood, where fashion sense means nothing more than clothes which don't itch.'

Though outspoken, increasingly so as she aged, Winwood was not outgoing, nor very self-promoting. 'One of the greatest self-promoters of all time was my dear friend Tallulah.' She paused as if to reflect, then warned, 'If you dare ask me Tallulah Who? I shall sack you!' She lapsed into a small smile and explained that during the Roaring Twenties, she and Bankhead had traded places: the American had gone to work on the English stage while the Englishwoman had come to work on the American stage.

'Tallulah, however, became a real star. I was a mere success. I was a star, off and on. She had looks, talent – I had both as well – but she also had charisma and a colossal nerve.' She summed up the incomparable Tallu thus: 'She was the all-time character. A dear, and a lady, but frequently most un-ladylike ... Oh, where to begin! I was the one person she could not shock. She said I was her anchor to sanity. That may have been stretching it a bit, but I think at times I did help to stabilize her ... She was always fun to be with, even though trying at times. She was always in the midst of a predicament, or about to create one.

'The sad part is, she had such a great natural talent, but settled for too little. She was crushed when she didn't make a hit in pictures. Then her biggest stage successes were made into pictures starring Bette Davis. She admired Davis, then later loathed her out of rivalry ... As Tallulah got older, she was terrified of losing her beauty. She was a brave pioneer, one of the first stars to have cosmetic surgery.

'She was born too soon, that's all. She was liberated when it was still shocking. By forty, her roles were nowhere as good, so she had to settle for mediocrity or repeat herself into a parody ... She did have a cult following, but cults are a trap. They don't let you change. She needed to mature. But she matured in an immature way.

'What killed her was excess. She drank too much and smoked too much. But her heart also broke – the theatre world had stopped thinking of her as a great talent, and once her looks went, talent was all she could cling to.'

In 1931 Estelle returned to London and the West End in *The Love Game*. 'I was approaching the half-century mark, and the roles had rather dried up in New York. They'd got too used to me, and I had to get used to more modest-sized characters ... In England, my good fortune in America meant I was warmly received. I was back in the fold, and all was smiles.'

She continued in plays until 1933, when she made her screen début in the British film *The House of Trent*. In the 1960s, Tallulah explained to *Motion Picture*, 'Estelle is the perfect proverbial little old lady, as far as the movies are concerned. If she wanted to, she could work every day of the year. She could corner the market in little old lady parts and then – scene-stealer that she is, and without lifting a thing except her eyelids – she could wipe all the other actresses off the screen!'

Nevertheless, until the 1950s, Winwood made only two films. The first, and *Quality Street*, with Katharine Hepburn: 'At the studio [RKO], they called her Katharine of Arrogance. Not without reason, as I could tell you – but why bother? I really have nothing to say about Miss Hepburn which you can print. Change the subject.'

By 1934, she was back in the States, dedicating herself to dozens of plays. She was Portia in *The Merchant of Venice* at the El Capitan in Hollywood in 1937. She played in *The*

Farmer Takes a Wife, toured in Coward's *To-Night at 8.30*, appeared in *The Merry Wives of Windsor* and found an autocratic niche in Wilde's *The Importance of Being Earnest* in 1939 as Lady Bracknell, a role to which she would return often.

Other credits included *Ladies in Retirement*, Coward's *Blithe Spirit* as Madame Arcati, *The Pirate*, Coward's *Hay Fever*, Agatha Christie's *Ten Little Indians*, Wilde's *Lady Windermere's fan*, Shaw's *Mrs Warren's Profession*, T.S. Eliot's *The Cocktail Party* and another Broadway triumph as the dotty Madame Constance in *The Madwoman of Chaillot* in 1949. She also performed and toured in Shakespeare. 'With or without the Bard, I was keeping English culture alive in America,' she winked.

'I was indefatigable then, frankly. I never considered my health, never listened to idiotic advice about slowing down. I've always done what I bloody well wanted.'

Among the scores of theatrical celebrities with whom she worked over the years were Alfred Lunt and Lynn Fontanne. 'I was in a play with them. Lynn was carrying on something frightful about her devotion to Alfred. Mostly for show, of course. It finally got on my nerves. One day, during a dress rehearsal, during the break, she wailed at me, wringing her hands, "Oh, where-oh-where would I be without Alfred?" I decided to tell her, for she wasn't getting any younger. I said, "You'd be right here, where I am – playing your mother." '

In the meantime, Winwood had married, more than once. Her first husband was Arthur Chesney, brother of British actor Edmund Gwenn (Kris Kringle in *Miracle on 34th Street*). Then stage director Guthrie McClintic, the homosexual husband of stage star Katharine Cornell. And New Zealand rancher Francis Barlow Bradley. In the late 1940s she wed English stage director and acting teacher Robert Henderson, but insiders said it too was a marriage in name only. Winwood eventually admitted in *Variety* that she rarely saw Henderson and that they lived in separate countries.

Her view of marriage? 'Somebody once said marriage is an institution, and who wants to live in an institution? I think it depends how you arrange your marriage. It depends, doesn't it?' As for children, she felt, 'Children have their place – in the nursery ... I prefer pets. They never outgrow you or outlive you, and they won't contest your will.'

Winwood's private life was off-limits to the press. She once warned an inquiring Fleet Street correspondent, 'Ask me no questions, and I shall tell you no lies.'

In 1956, after an absence of twenty-three years, the seventy-three-year-old returned to the London stage in *Gigi*, as Alicia de St Ephlam. 'The stupid thing about elderly characters is how little they're given to say.' Back in the US and Canada, she did such plays as *Speaking of Murder*, *Lute Song*, *The Circle*, *Madame Mousse*, and, on Broadway in 1966, *Nathan Weinstein, Mystic, Connecticut*. 'Some of the younger generations thought I was rather eerie. So I found myself in things having to do with murder and the like ... I was the lady who kept secrets.'

In the mid-1950s, she came back to the silver screen and carved out a second career as a film character actress. Perhaps most famously, she was Leslie Caron's fairy godmother in *The Glass Slipper* in 1954. 'I was rather good for costume pictures because I was from another era myself.'

She was featured in *The Swan* and *23 Paces to Baker Street*, both in 1956. The latter starred Van Johnson. 'He told me how lucky he'd been in becoming a star. It was the second major war. All the men stars were at war, and Van Johnson had a steel plate in his head, so they kept him in Hollywood. He himself volunteered this information. Nice fellow.'

Estelle was also seen in *Darby O'Gill and the Little People* (1959), and *The Misfits* (1961), the last film of both Clark Gable and Marilyn Monroe. 'Gable was very insecure. The first time he laid eyes upon you, he decided whether he liked you or not. More, I don't care to say.

'I liked *her*. She's so famous now, she doesn't require a name. Lovely child. Terribly insecure. I don't know what Gable's problem was, but she was still unhappy that she'd been born illegitimate – a very stupid word! I said to her there were many things worse than that. But I didn't want to make a list, didn't want to depress her further … She listened. Most younger stars, they don't listen. She did. I liked her rather a lot.'

Asked by me to describe some of her movie characters, the nonagenarian (about five feet tall) demurred. 'Pretty much the same,' she grinned wryly.

In 1962 she worked opposite another 1950s blonde, Kim Novak, in *The Notorious Landlady*. 'I liked her. She had that dreadful sex-pot image, but was more refined than that. I don't know she actually had charm, but she was nice and unspoilt … More recently, I admire her will-power. She lost her career, but kept her figure. It's ludicrous when a famous star packs on weight. If you are in the public eye, you owe it to yourself and to your public to look presentable.

'I may be a bag of bones, but I prefer it to a tub of lard. There is no good excuse for fat.'

Two years later, she enacted a formidable Pasadenan who takes Bette Davis to task in *Dead Ringer*. 'She loves being a star, and nobody around her is unaware of her status … A friend informed me that Ava Gardner ran into Miss Davis at a hotel in Madrid. I don't know when. But Miss Gardner was ecstatic. She told Davis she was a big fan of hers. Davis said, "Of course you are, my dear," and paraded on through the lobby.

'I worked with her. She played twins – both of them murderers, naturally – and I was a religious fanatic on her knees half the day. I think Miss Davis felt rather sorry for me because I had a small role. If so, it was a waste of her time. I'm more memorable in a small role than many stars in bigger ones. Fans tell me they remember my scenes better than the stars'.

'Miss Davis wasn't a tyrant, that I could see. But she had little time for niceties like "How do you do?" I don't blame her much, because she at least gave it her best. That's more than I can say for certain stars who smile out of one side of

their face, then curse their more talented co-stars or
supporting actors. Real talent excuses a lot of things.'

In 1965 Winwood was fleetingly seen in *Cat Ballou*,
starring Jane Fonda and Lee Marvin. In 1967 she rode
horseback in *Camelot*, starring Vanessa Redgrave. 'I was a
lady-in-waiting. As per usual. She was the prim queen in
front of the camera. Off camera, it was all go with her
political sloganeering and carryings-on with the Italian.' This
refers to Redgrave's affair with co-star Franco Nero, by
whom she had a child.

'In the olden days – which were not so good, but not so
scarlet, either – politics and affairs were kept entirely off the
set. A little hypocrisy goes a long way ...'

Also in 1967, at eight-four, the actress made love to Zero
Mostel in *The Producers*. 'Mr Mostel was an outsized man.
He had an outsized personality, a natural comic. A buffoon,
but elegant as well. He overcame numerous obstacles in his
life,' including the McCarthy blacklists, 'so I felt sorry for
him, having to do that dreadful picture. I can't bear to watch
it, even on a small television. I'm rather sorry I did it. I must
have needed the money – living in Hollywood weakens one's
motives.'

Of the cult film's creator, Mel Brooks, Winwood stated,
'He reminds me of the saying that nobody ever went broke
underestimating the American public's taste. Sad ... His first
films were his best. But that is not saying much.'

During the 1950s and especially the 1960s, the British
Californian also worked frequently on television. 'Somebody
said in my hearing – which is acute – that television is
nothing but rehearsals. I rather agree.' Among the shows she
brightened with her fey presence were *Playhouse 90, Dr
Kildare, Alfred Hitchcock Presents, Donna Reed, The Rogues,
Perry Mason, The FBI, Thriller* and *The Lucy Show*.

'Miss Ball was very nice to me. Eventually I heard she was
bloody rough on those younger than she was. But she was
nice to me. She always liked to see me sitting down. She
would lean over and ask me if all was well. I kept assuring

her that it was. I think she was afraid of old age, what it might do to her comedy and her looks. She probably looked at me and saw herself – if she were lucky and lived as long.

'She managed to get her way in everything. I rather admired that ... I was never a screamer. Tallulah was. It's bloody effective. Instead, I merely walk away from unpleasantness – good for your blood pressure, I suppose. It depends what one wants: a big career or a long life.'

Winwood took part in small-screen productions of *Miss Mabel*, *Blithe Spirit* as Madame Arcati, and *Great Expectations* as Miss Havisham. She dourly observed that she seldom got to originate significant roles once she passed 'seventy or thereabouts', but that casting directors eventually saw her in 'all the classic elderly roles for ladies'.

She declined hatchet-murderess roles out of her aversion to violence, but frankly noted, 'The loony roles are usually for the central character. They're usually offered to Miss Davis or the Crawford woman.' Asked her opinion of Joan, she grimly shook her head. 'No comment. I saw her once at her very worst. I do not condone sadism.'

The Englishwoman preferred 'campy, cartoon-like violence' to explicit gore. She was thus well-suited to *Batman*, on which series she guested more than once. She said of Cesar Romero, who played The Joker, 'I suggested he write his memoirs. Everybody does. Most do it rather boringly or lie about the whole thing. Cesar said he would rather leave it all unchronicled. It's a pity. He knows all the secrets and the skeletons too.

'Whenever publishers come to me on unbended knee, they insult me. Unwittingly, I hope. They say what they really want is the inside on X, Y and Z. People – big stars – I've worked with. They're especially keen to have the dirt on Tallulah, and I could never do that. I'd feel I was betraying a trust. For money. Spite would be a good reason – not money – and I never had cause to spite Tallulah. So I tell the publishers to go to hell.'

Ms Winwood admitted to continuing to work for the

'relief from boredom' and sometimes for money's sake. Her philosophy was that too little money was a problem, and so was too much. She liked having 'enough in the bank for the next five years ... But when you live this long, you require that much more money. I mustn't discuss it further, though, it's not lady-like.'

A continuing secondary role on a TV series could have made Estelle that much more famous, and financially secure for even her lifetime. However, she wasn't 'social enough. I do not travel the cocktail party circuit.' Instead, she kept to a small circle of friends who visited her home in Los Angeles' San Fernando Valley and played bridge three or more times a week. She also was too old to be insurable in a recurring series role.

'The unions were a good idea. Then they went overboard. Now, regulations abound – too much ... Everything is money. It's insurance. It's too much pampering the spoiled artiste.' At eighty-three Estelle complained in an interview that under union rules, rehearsals could not exceed seven consecutive hours.

Another casting 'problem' was her nationality and her upper-crust voice and image. 'They tend to explain me away as a countess or somebody's rich great-aunt. They use more lines of dialogue explaining who I am than they give me to say!'

In her late eighties, she finally began slowing down. With the 1970s, youth was more *in* than ever, and roles for elderly women were exceedingly scarce on big or small screens. What little theatre existed in Hollywood focused on youth, and had a larger role come her way, 'Too many lines would have been a bother to memorize ... Theatre is for younger actors. Once you reach eighty or so, it's time to sit in the audience ... if the play doesn't put you to sleep.'

Nineteen-seventy-six was a landmark year for Estelle Winwood. She returned to movies in the all-star comedy hit *Murder By Death*. The alphabetical cast was heavy on Brits:

Alec Guinness, Elsa Lanchester, David Niven, Peter Sellers, Maggie Smith and Winwood. Also Eileen Brennan, Truman Capote, James Coco, Peter Falk and Nancy Walker. Estelle played the aged nurse-in-a-wheelchair to Lanchester's Jessica Marbles, a take-off of Agatha Christie's Jane Marple. At the time, Winwood, ninety-three, was listed as the oldest working member of the Screen Actors Guild.

Her role she blithely characterized as 'an old lady – a bit cliché, but there you are'.

She described three of her co-stars:

Truman Capote. 'Like Katharine Hepburn – arrogant. But not half so pretty, or thin. Underneath, he wants to be liked. But he's got the warmth of an alligator ... The press was always fawning over him. Because it's his first motion picture, I suppose. It may be his last. He's not a fine actor; he plays himself, and you can get that on television for free.

'It's not so bad, being yourself. If it's a rather interesting self. I'm usually myself, unless they ask me to be somebody else or the dialogue mandates that I be different. If they don't ask, I don't bother.

'Mr Capote was always gossiping on the set, and he hasn't met half the interesting people I have! He probably never heard a piece of good news in his life – or wouldn't admit to it. He rather reminds me of Somerset Maugham.'

Maggie Smith. 'Most lady stars you can name have got better with age. Maggie Smith, for example. Far less interesting in the 1960s, wasn't it? I'm not sure if she was dull then, or simply marooned in dull parts. Then she did that Scottish thing [the 1968 film *The Prime of Miss Jean Brodie*], and ever since, she's been outstanding. Even in smaller parts, and all of ours were in *Murder By Death*.'

Elsa Lanchester. 'Not a friendly woman, and rather daft. Except when I saw her around her husband [Charles Laughton, who died in 1962]. Then, she was simply dull ... If she'd stayed in England, she'd have starved. She came here and made a living playing English eccentrics. It wasn't talent – it's her being herself, and she's got barmier with the years.

'I was in a wheelchair, so she ignored me most of the time. *She* was playing a famous *author* ... Probably didn't like anyone who came from where she did – competition. She'd go around telling everybody about the few famous people she'd known, like Laughton mostly and Isadora Duncan and God knows what other fossils ... It's not nice to ignore your [scenes] partner.'

Winwood also appraised some of her fellow great dames:

Edith Evans. 'A very nice lady. I can't tell you much about her as an actress. I can say I've heard she's rather good. Or very good, depending. I don't follow people's careers, you see. I'd rather read or play cards than keep up with the latest trends, most of which are dull.'

Hermione Gingold. 'The last time I saw her, she snubbed me. Cut me dead. I said so to a friend of mine. My friend said it must have been because *I* stayed thin ...'

Joan Greenwood. 'A lot of the local [British] actresses who achieved fame in the pictures were weak as water. Miss Greenwood had an edge to her. I like that. She was the best thing in *Kind Hearts and Coronets*. They all praised Alec Guinness. He's a talented ham. Who wouldn't seize the chance to play sixteen (*sic*) roles in one picture? In pictures, that's easy. They're not as wearying as the stage – that's *real* work.'

Beatrice Lillie. 'I politely suggested that she might experiment with a new hairstyle, something less boyish. She took offence, said I shouldn't interfere in her private life. The cheek of it! I was merely commenting on her bloody hair.'

Celia Johnson. 'The luckiest actress of her day, because she was given the chance to shine in *Brief Encounter*. It wasn't all luck, of course, because she did it perfectly. Thank goodness they didn't put a real star in it. Big stars usually ruin everything they touch. Including their fans.'

Margaret Rutherford. 'She made me laugh, so I rather liked her. She didn't make fun of others, like today's comics. She was good at that type of thing she did, quite good. I'm afraid that's probably what they say about me. In entertainment, they praise with one side of their mouth, and qualify it with the other.

'Funny, about both Margaret Rutherford and Margaret Hamilton [best known as the Wicked Witch of the West in *The Wizard of Oz*]. Both were dreadfully plain in their youth. The older they got, the easier they were to look at ... Age brings down great beauties, but it's also an equalizer – it makes ugly young women into nice-looking old ladies. Time does heal some wounds. For some people.'

Though *Murder By Death* brought Winwood back into the public gaze, it was also 1976 in which she broke her hip and had to give up tennis, as well as work for some time. 'Health is like the weather. It's best when you don't have to deal with it.' Increasingly, she had to cut down on reading, as her eyesight diminished. 'I love books. Most of my entertainment for some decades has been books. And of course cards.'

Now and again, Estelle was invited on to TV talk shows, as much for her age as to reminisce about Tallulah and Others. 'Nobody remembers the plays I was in – starred in. They know the movies – movies and television, it's all that matters to people under forty. Do you read? Well, you would, you're a writer, and writing's the other side of reading.

'But if people only read fiction, then it's almost as useless as watching the television.'

At nearly a hundred, the actress made her final appearance on an episode of the Jack Klugman series *Quincy* which aired in the 1982-3 TV season.

At a hundred, she was thrust into the limelight again, more firmly than ever. She received letters and telegrams from stars, heads of state and Queen Elizabeth II. When the media came to interview her, she found the sudden attention and curiosity unnerving. To one man who asked her how it felt turning one hundred, she snapped, 'How rude of you to remind me of my age!' To another, she replied, 'Who wants to be a hundred?' asked if it weren't preferable to death, she answered, 'I wouldn't mind being dead. It would be something new.'

Solicited for her advice on longevity, she crisply replied that she had avoided the sun for her complexion but had never done much to prolong her life. She still smoked 'too much' and enjoyed sherry. She allowed that she often played bridge with her actor friends until two in the morning, then watched television till dawn. 'I do what I like and what I'm able.'

I asked Estelle in person how she'd balanced her career and personal life. At first she misunderstood the somewhat modern question. Then she waved her hand dismissively, prior to lighting a cigarette. 'I never tried to balance anything. Just live my life. Personal, professional, impersonal … it's all mixed in together.' After a few puffs, she confessed: 'It doesn't take very long to realize whether an actor will be a huge success or not. I was successful and I had very nice looks. But I realized when young that there was no special place reserved for me in the heavens. I became a working actress … It takes much more time to know if your personal life will be a success. It's easier-going with friends than lovers. Sex spoils most relationships. After my first disappointment or two, I simply decided not to give it that much importance.

'People can disappoint you, but work is always there. Potentially. It gets you through, when relationships threaten to do the opposite … So why would I try and balance anything? Or even want to sacrifice my work to somebody?'

Insiders said that Estelle's long career kept her vitally interested, in life and other people. Actors, she frequently stated, were 'an interesting lot' to be around.

In time, she had to make the move to the Motion Picture & Television Country Home & Hospital in Woodland Hills, near Los Angeles. Surrounded by former actors, all reportedly younger than herself, Estelle Winwood passed away in June 1984, five months after her hundred-and-first birthday. She was buried in an unmarked grave at Westwood

Memorial Cemetery, blocks away from several of Los Angeles' première movie houses. The same cemetery holds the remains of co-stars Marilyn Monroe and Truman Capote.

On two separate occasions, I asked Estelle what she wanted on her theoretical tombstone. She answered slightly differently each time. Both epitaphs would have been appropriate for a great dame:

'*She did as she pleased*' and '*She did and she pleased.*'